UNDERSTANDING ETERNAL
SECURITY

UNDERSTANDING ETERNAL

SECURITY

CHARLES
STANLEY

THOMAS NELSON PUBLISHERS
Nashville

Copyright © 1998 by Charles Stanley

All rights reserved. Written permission must be secured from the publisher to use or reproduce any part of this book, except for brief quotations in critical reviews or articles.

Published in Nashville, Tennessee, by Thomas Nelson, Inc.

The Bible version used in this publication is THE NEW KING JAMES VERSION. Copyright © 1979, 1980, 1982, Thomas Nelson, Inc., Publishers.

ISBN 0-7852-7283-6

Printed in the United States of America

CONTENTS

Introduction: You Can Know with Certainty!   vii

1. Getting God's Perspective on Eternal Security   1
2. The Nature of Your Salvation   9
3. Why It Is Important for You to Believe in Eternal Security   21
4. Seven Reasons for Believing in Eternal Security: Part 1   33
5. Seven Reasons for Believing in Eternal Security: Part 2   43
6. Solemn Warnings: Part 1   54
7. Solemn Warnings: Part 2   64
8. A License to Sin?   75
9. Eternal Rewards   86
10. Living in the Assurance of Eternal Security   98

Conclusion: Eternally Secure and *Free*!   108

INTRODUCTION

YOU CAN KNOW WITH CERTAINTY!

Every time we offer a tape series on eternal security, the response is overwhelming. I am always amazed at the great number of people who are interested in this topic, and who apparently do not have the absolute assurance that they are saved. Many of these people are believers in Christ Jesus and have had a genuine salvation experience, yet they do not know with *certainty* that they will go to heaven when they die.

Essentially there are five categories of people in our world today:

1. Those who are unsaved and know they are unsaved. They have no security regarding their eternal future.
2. Those who are unsaved but think they are saved. They have a false security about eternity.
3. Those who are saved but are uncertain about whether they are saved. They are insecure.
4. Those who believe they were saved in the past, or even present, but who are unsure about their salvation in eternity. They have a feeling of security in the here and now, but they are not "eternally" secure.
5. Those who are certain that they have been saved, are saved, and will be saved forever. They are the ones who truly are "eternally secure" in their salvation experience.

It is my great hope that by the time you complete this study, you will be among that last category of believers in Christ Jesus—knowing that you are saved forever by your personal acceptance of what Jesus did for you on the cross.

Falling from Grace

The opposite belief regarding eternal security is one generally called "falling from grace." According to this position, a person can "lose" his or her salvation through sin and wayward living after a salvation experience. I once argued this viewpoint very strongly.

What caused me to become a firm believer in the truth of eternal security? While I was in seminary, working on a particular passage of the New Testament in a Greek course, I had one of those irrefutable "dawning of the truth" experiences in my life. I saw clearly that a person can have a *sure* understanding of *eternal* security and a destiny that is forever linked to that of Jesus Christ. I began to search the Scriptures in earnest, reading everything I could to compare the two approaches. I no longer was trying to prove my earlier position that a person might "fall from grace," and neither was I doubting the new insight I had into the Scriptures. In effect, I was in a neutral position.

The more I studied *all* of the passages of the New Testament that deal with eternal security, sin, and grace, the more I saw that God, indeed, provides eternal security for those who believe in Jesus Christ.

Most Christians, I have found, do not truly study this topic—rather, they cling to whatever position they were taught as children. When we accept without genuine *understanding* the tenets of our faith, we can easily be led into error. Certainly, I am not asking you to doubt all that you have learned about God, Jesus Christ, the Holy Spirit, or the Bible. Far from it! Rather, I am asking you to *look for yourself* into the depths of the Scriptures on this topic and gain an understanding that is born of your own study.

A Baptist Doctrine?

Many people associate the topic of eternal security with a doctrinal position of "once saved, always saved." In turn, they associate this doctrine with Baptists, as well as several other denominations. The fact of the matter is, however, that eternal security is not a doctrinal issue—it is a matter of biblical truth. This Bible study is just that, a *Bible* study, not a doctrinal study.

I encourage you to fully investigate this topic before you draw a firm conclusion about eternal security. Be careful not to condemn before you investigate. As has been said by many through the ages, "Condemnation before investigation leads to error."

I believe that as you look into God's Word with an open heart, eager for the truth to be revealed to you by the Holy Spirit—whom Jesus called the Spirit of Truth—you will find a genuine peace for your soul. If you are not genuinely born again, I pray that this study will lead you to accept Jesus Christ as your Savior. If you are born again, then I trust this study will lead you to place an even greater confidence in what Jesus Christ purchased for you with His shed blood. If you are doubting your salvation, or questioning your eternal destiny as a born-again believer, I trust this study will settle your doubts once and for all.

The fact on which this entire study is based is this: You can know with assurance that Jesus Christ is your Savior *forever*.

GETTING GOD'S PERSPECTIVE ON ETERNAL SECURITY

Each of us has a unique perspective on life. We have a distinct way of looking at things, judging things, and holding things in our memories. Our perspective is something we have learned, and therefore, it is something that changes as we "relearn" or "learn more" about life.

In my years of ministry, I have found that a wrong perspective is very common when it comes to the matter of personal salvation. Many have misconceptions about how they became born again—they err in their understanding about the basis for their salvation. Consequently, it is very easy for them to misunderstand how they might "lose" their salvation. They do not understand why God forgives, what it means to be saved, or how to live within the fullness of their salvation.

To gain the right perspective on eternal security, we must go to God's Word and stay there. The Bible is God's foremost communication to us on this topic. It is the reference to which we must return continually if we are to truly understand what has happened to us spiritually in a born-again experience, and to understand fully what that experience means for all eternity.

Facing the truth, especially if it differs from the way we have been raised, can be difficult. It means a major shift in our understanding of the world and of the way life "works." It means a shift in our understanding of God and His relationship with us. Yet we must be willing to face the truth if we are truly to live in the spiritual freedom that God desires for us. We must face squarely the fact that any time our perspective does not match up with God's eternal truth, we err . . . and error, when clung to and used as a basis for decisions and relationships, can lead to sin or spiritual bondage.

As you work your way through this study, I strongly encourage you to keep your Bible at your side. As you study each passage noted in this booklet, make notes in the margins of your Bible. Read the passage from Scripture for yourself. It is far more important that you write God's insights into your Bible than to write them in this booklet, although places are provided for you to make notes.

Keys to This Study

You will be asked at various points in this booklet to respond to the material presented by answering one or more of these questions:

- What new insights have you gained?
- Have you ever had a similar experience?
- How do you feel about this?
- In what way are you feeling challenged to change your thinking or to take action?

Insights

A spiritual insight occurs when you read a passage from the Bible and the meaning of that passage suddenly seems crystal clear to you—you have a new or clearer understanding of God's Word that is undeniable. It is as if God suddenly draws back the curtain to reveal to you a new level or depth of meaning. You truly *know* what you know!

Insights happen to all who read the Word, even to those who may have read and studied a particular passage for countless years. I encourage you to ask God to give you insights every time you read His Word. I believe that is a prayer He delights in answering.

Insights are usually very personal, and they nearly always relate to your experiences in life, either current or past. Insights are related to how you might *apply* God's Word in a way that is always timely, yet at the same time eternal.

Note your insights. You'll find three great advantages in this: First, you will be able to review your insights later in the light of still other Scriptures that you study. Second, you will have your insights readily available should an opportunity arise to share or discuss them with others. And third, you will tend to experience even more insights if you are looking and listening for them in a focused, intentional way. As Jesus taught, when we *seek*, we find. (See Matt. 7:7.)

Periodically in this study, you will be asked to note what specific passages of the Bible are saying to you. This is your opportunity to record insights.

Experiences

Everything you read in God's Word is, to a degree, filtered by your past experiences. You no doubt have said to yourself or others on a number of occasions, "I know that particular truth in the Bible is real because of what happened to me."

The more we see the Bible as relating to our personal experiences, the more the Bible confirms, encourages, convicts, challenges, and transforms us. We come to the place where we see that God's Word is universal—as well as personal and individual—and that there isn't anything we experience as human beings that isn't addressed by the Bible in one or more ways. The Bible is about people and God's relationship to people. The Bible tells us how God works in and through experiences to communicate with people. Certainly as we look back on history, we can see that human nature has not changed. The details related to technology may differ, but the human heart remains the same. What people experienced in Bible times, people also experience today.

Now, I am not advocating a purely "experiential" basis for faith or believing in God's Word. What I am saying is this: the Bible is filled with stories that tell the *experiences* of men and women who were just like you. The Bible teaches how to deal with life's experiences. If you do not have a personal story that relates to a specific passage, in all likelihood you know somebody who has such a personal story, or you *will* have a personal story that is related to it in the future.

The advantage to noting your experiences is that you gain a new understanding about how God has dealt with you throughout your life to bring you to the place where you are today, and your faith is strengthened to trust God to be with you in the future.

The advantage to sharing your experiences as they relate to the Bible is that you will grow spiritually as you share your faith with others. Your personal witness will become stronger and you will be more at ease in sharing what Christ has done for you, in you, and through you. Even if you are doing this study on your own, I encourage you to talk to others about your faith experiences.

Emotional Responses

Just as we each have a unique set of experiences, so we also have a unique emotional response to God's Word. No one emotional response is more valid or "right" than another. You may be frightened or puzzled by something you read, and the person next to you in your study group may feel joy or relief after reading the same passage.

Face your emotional responses honestly. Learn to share your emotions with others.

Keep in mind, however, that neither your experiences nor your emotional responses make the Bible true. The Bible is truth, period. The value in looking at our experiences and our emotional responses lies in our gaining greater understanding of how the Bible might be *applied* to our lives.

Why are emotions worthy of exploration? Because the Bible always has an emotional impact on us. We simply cannot read it without having some kind of emotional response to it. Sometimes we are moved to tears by what we read. At other times we may feel great elation, sorrow, conviction, hope, longing, surprise, love . . . and yes, even anger and indignation. When we take a look at our own feelings, we often see more clearly what the Lord is desiring to do in us and how He may desire for us to pursue an additional avenue of study. For example, if you are puzzled by what you read, and you recognize that you are puzzled, you will likely want to know why you feel that way. Your emotional response can lead you to seek out answers that you may not originally have intended to pursue.

Allow the Scriptures to touch your heart. God created you with emotions. He knows that you feel certain ways toward Him, toward others, and toward His Word. What He desires is that you are in touch with your feelings. He knows how you feel. He wants *you* to know how you feel.

As you meet with others, you will find that it is far more advantageous to a group study to share emotional responses than to share "opinions" or "ideas." Don't allow yourselves to become sidetracked by opinions. Commentaries and scholarly facts have their place, but ultimately, the Bible is a spiritual book that reflects the unfathomable riches of God's own Spirit. Emotions are often very close to reflecting a genuine *spiritual* response.

The topic of eternal security is certainly one that is laden with emotions for most people. Some are afraid of their eternal fate, others are joyous about the destiny they believe God has for them. Some are puzzled about God's truth on this subject; others may feel conviction or even sorrow related to what they read about eternal life. Allow all of these emotional responses to exist freely in your group. You will have a far richer study experience. You very likely will find yourself "bonding" in a way that a sharing of opinions simply does not generate.

Be aware, at the same time, that this topic might easily cause a Bible study group to turn into a feel-good, group-therapy type of session. Don't allow that to happen. Stay in the Word.

The tendency of some regarding eternity and those who are doubting or feeling conviction about their own spiritual state is to say, "Oh, don't worry. You'll be all right." That is a wonderful response to give to a person who truly is born again . . . but it is a disastrous response to give to a person who has not truly been saved. Be aware that there may be those in your midst who are not saved or who do not know with certainty that they have been saved. Give them an opportunity to come to Christ *as they read and study the Word and the Holy Spirit deals with their hearts.* Don't press them to this decision; at the same time, do not deny them the opportunity to experience Christ's salvation of their souls.

Challenges

God always intends for us to be challenged in some way by His Word. He has a purpose in communicating with us—our spiritual growth and transformation in the likeness of Jesus Christ. Since none of us have been fully transformed, we all have room to grow, and therefore, God will continue to challenge us even though we may have been a born-again believer for many years.

Real growth does not come simply by knowing or understanding God's Word, but rather by applying it to our daily lives. As you read and study God's Word, identify as best you can those areas in which you believe God is challenging you, stretching you, or causing you to trust Him in new ways. A topic such as eternal security may seem to relate only to your heavenly future. In fact, it is a topic that has direct relevance and application to your life *today*—in the here and now. What you believe about your future will have a direct bearing on how you live your life, and especially on how you share the gospel with others.

God desires to get you into His Word for one main purpose—so He can get His Word into you. The Word will change your life, your thinking, your decisions, your outlook. It will also compel you to share God's Word with others. Always be alert for opportunities to discuss the things you are learning in this study. Some of those opportunities may appear suddenly or even seem coincidental. From God's perspective, however, these opportunities are divine appointments. The greater your understanding of eternal life and the security of your salvation, the more of God's truth you will have to share with those who are unsaved, without hope, or wavering in their commitment to follow Christ. Do not be surprised when God brings such people across your path—you now have a life-giving message to share with them! Be bold in your witness.

If you do not have somebody with whom you can discuss your insights, experiences, emotions, and challenges, find somebody. You may feel led to start a Bible study in your home. You may want to talk to your pastor about organizing a Bible study group in your church. There is much you can learn on your own. There is much more to be learned as you become part of a small group that desires to grow in the Lord and to understand His Word more fully.

Keep the Bible Central

Again, I encourage you to keep the Bible central to your study. Come to God's Word as if it were a great banquet table from which you can eat until the hunger of your soul is fully satisfied.

If you are doing a personal Bible study, be diligent in keeping your focus on God's Word. Self-analysis or gaining insight so you might judge others is *not* the goal. Becoming more like Jesus Christ, stronger in your witness for Him, and more certain of your eternal future—these are the goals.

Prayer

Finally, I encourage you to begin and end each Bible study session in prayer. Ask God to give you spiritual ears to hear what He wants you to hear and spiritual eyes to see what He wants you to see. Request that He give you new insights into His Word, bringing to your mind experiences that relate to what you read. Ask Him to help you identify and clarify your emotions as He reveals to you what He desires for you to be, say, and do in response to His Word.

As you end a Bible study session, ask the Lord to plant His Word in your heart so that it might take root and grow and bear fruit. Petition Him to transform you into the likeness of Jesus Christ. Ask Him to show you ways in which to apply the Scriptures to your daily life. Pray for courage to act upon what He is calling you to do, and to be bold in your witness to the gospel.

- *What new insights about eternal security do you hope to gain from this study? Is there a burning question in your soul that you desire to have answered?*

  _____

  _____

- *Have you struggled in the past with the issue of eternal security? Have you experienced God's forgiveness in your life? Have you come to a full understanding and assurance about your heavenly home and eternal destiny?*

  _____

  _____

- *How to you feel about eternity?*

  _____

  _____

- *Are you open to the possibility that God desires for you to experience a confident assurance about your eternal security?*

  _____

  _____

- *Do you feel comfortable telling others about heaven and life eternal? Do you feel comfortable assuring others of their salvation and their eternal home with the Lord?*

  _____

  _____

THE NATURE OF YOUR SALVATION

As we begin our study of eternal security, we must keep two definitions very clearly in mind:

Salvation—Deliverance from eternal death, and possession of eternal life.

Eternal Security—That work of God which guarantees God's gift of salvation, once received, is possessed forever and can never be lost.

What you believe and know about these two terms is vital to your hope and confidence as a Christian, as well as to your witness for Christ. *Confusion about how you were saved leads to confusion about how a person might remain saved.*

What It Means to Be "Saved"

To be saved from sin's consequences is *not* synonymous with:

- Dropping bad behaviors and adopting good ones in order to "get right with God"
- Joining a church
- Deciding to call yourself a Christian
- Going to the altar and saying you are sorry for your sins
- Changing your bad habits
- Adding Christian disciplines such as prayer or Bible reading to your daily routine

All of these things are "works" of some kind. Salvation comes by *faith*. Salvation is the result of believing, not a by-product of doing.

Nicodemus, a very religious man in the time of Jesus, was shocked when Jesus told him that the good works he had done as a Law-keeping Jew were inadequate for his being born again spiritually. Read what Jesus said to Nicodemus:

> Most assuredly, I say to you, unless one is born of water and the Spirit, he cannot enter the kingdom of God. That which is born of the flesh is flesh, and that which is born of the Spirit is spirit. Do not marvel that I said to you, "You must be born again." The wind blows where it wishes, and you hear the sound of it, but cannot tell where it comes from and where it goes. So is everyone who is born of the Spirit.
>
> . . . As Moses lifted up the serpent in the wilderness, even so must the Son of Man be lifted up, that whoever believes in Him should not perish but have eternal life. For God so loved the world that He gave His only begotten Son, that whoever believes in Him should not perish but have everlasting life. For God did not send His Son into the world to condemn the world, but that the world through Him might be saved. He who believes in Him is not condemned; but he who does not believe is condemned already, because he has not believed in the name of the only begotten Son of God (John 3:5–8, 14–18).

• *Based upon the teaching and experience you have had in the past, what does it mean to you to be "saved" from sin?*

_____

_____

• *What new insights do you have into this passage of Scripture from the Gospel of John?*

_____

_____

The Root Problem of a Sin Nature

To believe in eternal security is not to deny the fact that man has a sin problem or that sin bears consequences, including the potential consequence of eternal death. Jesus made it very clear to Nicodemus that mankind has a sin problem. Furthermore, that sin problem puts mankind into the status of being "condemned already" (John 3:18). People *can* perish and be separated from God eternally if they do not face their sin problem and receive God's provision for it. Jesus spoke very clearly about this in Matthew 25:

- "Cast the unprofitable servant into the outer darkness. There will be weeping and gnashing of teeth" (v. 30).
- "He will also say to those on the left hand, 'Depart from Me, you cursed, into the everlasting fire prepared for the devil and his angel's" (v. 41).
- "These will go away into everlasting punishment, but the righteous into eternal life" (v. 46).

Sin against God is going beyond the boundaries established by God. It is not only a behavioral problem, however—one rooted in attitudes, motives, actions, and patterns of conduct. It is a "nature" problem, an identity or "state of being" problem. Man's sin nature is one of pride, greed, and total self-centeredness and self-will. Every person is born with this sin nature. Behavior is learned; our natural tendency to sin is not. A sin nature is inherent, and it is inherent regardless of the spiritual condition of our parents. It is part of our inheritance as fallen human beings, the descendants of Adam and Eve.

Now, a person might change his or her behavior as an act of the will. But a person cannot change his or her basic sin nature, regardless of how much "willpower" is exerted. We are incapable of transforming our spirits or of altering the core of our spiritual being. We are born with a "sin condition" that only God can correct.

The good news is that while we were in this helpless, ungodly state, God sent His Son, Jesus, to die for us so that we do not have to experience the consequence of our sin nature—which is separation and alienation from God. We *can* be transformed and made new in spirit.

What the Word Says	What the Word Says to Me
And you He made alive, who were dead in trespasses and sins, in which you once walked according to the course of this world, according to the prince of the power of the air, the spirit who now works in the sons of disobedience, among whom also we all once conducted ourselves in the lusts of our flesh, fulfilling the desires of the flesh and of the mind, and were by nature children of wrath, just as the others (Eph. 2:1–3).	----------------- ----------------- ----------------- ----------------- ----------------- ----------------- ----------------- ----------------- ----------------- ----------------- ----------------- ----------------- ----------------- -----------------
For when we were still without strength, in due time Christ died for the ungodly. . . . God demonstrates His own love toward us, in that while we were still sinners, Christ died for us. . . . For if when we were enemies we were reconciled to God through the death of His Son, much more, having been reconciled, we shall be saved by His life (Rom. 5:6, 8, 10).	----------------- ----------------- ----------------- ----------------- ----------------- ----------------- ----------------- ----------------- ----------------- ----------------- ----------------- -----------------

God's Provision for Man's Sin Problem

God has a "provision" for man's sin problem—a provision born of His love. Every man and woman is the object of God's love, regardless of their past or present deeds. It is wrong, however, to conclude that every person is "accepted" or has been made acceptable to God. Even though God loves each person with an immeasurable, unfathomable love, God's pure and holy nature cannot coexist with sin. In order for man and God to be fully reconciled, the nature of man must be changed from a sin (wrong) nature to a righteous (right) nature. Only when this transformation has been made and a man or woman has been "born again" in spirit by the Spirit is that person accepted as being in right standing with God.

Many people in our world today wrongly conclude that because God loves everybody, surely He will save everybody—in other words, nobody will be punished for entering eternity with an untransformed sin nature. That is not what the Bible teaches. Jesus made it very clear that sin has consequences, including eternal consequences, but that just as surely, God has made a provision for the sin nature of man to be changed. Man must act on that provision if he is to avoid the punishment reserved for those who enter eternity with an unchanged sin nature.

Believing and Receiving

Jesus told Nicodemus that the "receiving" of God's provision is a simple matter of believing. Jesus said, "Whoever believes in Him should not perish but have everlasting life" (John 3:16).

Jesus further told Nicodemus the basis on which Nicodemus must believe: "As Moses lifted up the serpent in the wilderness, even so must the Son of Man be lifted up" (John 3:14). "Lifted up" was a reference to Jesus being raised upon a cross of crucifixion, on which Jesus would die for the sins of mankind.

Read again the story in the Old Testament to which Jesus referred:

> The people spoke against God and against Moses. . . . So the LORD sent fiery serpents among the people, and they bit the people; and many of the people of Israel died. Therefore the people came to Moses, and said, "We have sinned, for we have spoken against the LORD and against you; pray to the LORD that He take away the serpents from us." So Moses prayed for the people. Then the LORD said to Moses, "Make a fiery serpent, and set it on a pole; and it shall be that everyone who is bitten, when he looks at it, shall live." So Moses made a bronze serpent, and put it on a pole; and

so it was, if a serpent had bitten anyone, when he looked at the bronze serpent, he lived (Num. 21:5–9).

Note clearly that *all* the Israelites had to do was to *look* upon the serpent (with belief that this was God's provision for their deliverance) in order for the Israelites to be cured of the consequences of their sin. Jesus said this same pattern would hold true for those who "looked" upon His death on the cross. All a person needs to do today in order to be saved from the consequences of their sin nature is to look at Jesus on the cross, believing that Jesus was and is forever God's sole provision for man's sin problem. A belief in Jesus as God's Son and as God's sacrifice for the sins of man is what saves a person. *Nothing less will do, but nothing more is required.*

What Does It Mean to "Believe"?

Believing in Jesus does not mean that a person merely believes that Jesus once lived on this earth, or that He was a good man or a fine religious teacher. Believing in Jesus means to place one's trust in Jesus as the provision of God for the forgiveness of sin. It means believing Jesus was, indeed, God's only begotten Son who paid the debt for *your* sin and who therefore qualifies to be *your* Savior. Believing in Jesus means believing that Jesus' death on the cross was

- *substitutionary*—in your place; on account of your sin.
- *atoning*—for the forgiveness of your sin, making it possible for you to be restored to God and accepted by Him.
- *sacrificial*—the shedding of His blood instituted a new covenant relationship between you and God.

All who believe in the substitutionary, atoning, sacrificial death of Jesus are *saved*. That is what it means to be saved.

- *How do you feel when you read verses from the Bible related to the consequences of unforgiven sin?*

_____

_____

• *How do you feel when you read verses from the Bible related to God's provision for the forgiveness of sin's consequences?*

_____

_____

God's Promises Related to God's Provision

Any person who believes and receives fully the provision that God made in Jesus Christ's death on the cross is a person who automatically receives two "promises." One promise is related to a *quantity* of life, the other to a new *quality* of life.

An Everlasting Quantity of Life

Jesus told Nicodemus this about His death on the cross: "Whoever believes . . . should not perish but have everlasting life" (John 3:16). In many versions of the Bible the word *should* in this verse is translated "will" or "shall." The intent of Jesus is that whoever believes will *undeniably* be given everlasting life by God. There are no qualifiers to this promise—no ifs, ands, or buts.

The promise of a heavenly home was also made by Jesus in John 14:

> Let not your heart be troubled; you believe in God, believe also in Me. In My Father's house are many mansions; if it were not so, I would have told you. I go to prepare a place for you. And if I go and prepare a place for you, I will come again and receive you to Myself; that where I am, there you may be also. And where I go you know, and the way you know (vv. 1–4).

A New Quality of Life

Jesus also gave a promise related to the quality of a person's life once he or she has accepted God's provision of Jesus' sacrificial death. Jesus said that upon believing in Him, a person is "birthed" by the Holy Spirit. Read again what Jesus said to Nicodemus: "That which is born of the Spirit is spirit" (John 3:6). When you accept Jesus as your Savior and believe in His death on the cross as being *your* provision for forgiveness, the Spirit causes your spirit to be reborn or made new.

Note two very important things about this rebirth by the Spirit:

1. *The Spirit does the birthing.* You cannot will for it to be done. Your part is to look upon the Cross and believe in Jesus as your provision for forgiveness by God. God's part is to bring about the transformation of your spiritual nature.

2. *Once a person has received the Holy Spirit into his or her life, that person will have a desire to love God, serve God, and walk in the ways of God.* The person who has been truly born anew will want to live according to God's commandments and to follow the daily leading of the Holy Spirit. The giving of the Holy Spirit is to help us walk in this new way of life.

What About Repentance?

The word *repent* means to have a change of mind. The Holy Spirit dwelling within a person will cause a person to want to have a change of mind, and therefore, a subsequent change of behavior. Repentance comes in the wake of salvation.

Let me give you an example of this. A man might have a change of mind about whether smoking is the right thing to do. He might begin to believe that smoking is harmful to his physical health and make a decision to change his behavior. In effect, he has "repented" of smoking. But this does not mean that this man is saved spiritually. Nothing about the person's sin nature has been altered . . . only his behavior when it comes to smoking.

Many people walk down church aisles to kneel at altars and repent of behaviors that they know are bad or sinful in God's eyes. They repent of adulterous affairs, selfish actions, hateful words and deeds, and countless other deeds of their past. They believe that by admitting their sins and making a promise to God that they are going to do "better" in the future, they are then "saved." In reality, nothing has happened to them spiritually because they have not truly accepted and believed in Jesus as their sole means of salvation from the consequences of their sin nature. They may be confessing their sins, asking for forgiveness, and repenting, but they are not necessarily believing in and receiving Jesus Christ. A person can say, "I'm sorry, please forgive me, I don't ever want to do this again," and never say with genuine belief, "I believe in and accept what Jesus Christ did on the cross as being for my sins. I receive Him as my Savior."

When these people leave the altar—having repented but not having truly been saved—they attempt to change their old behavioral patterns and habits. When they slip and fall back into their old habits, they think they are no longer saved. Nothing could be farther from the truth, for indeed, they never *were* saved. They had merely tried to change their behavior, and whether they acknowledge it to be true or not, they were hoping to get "good enough" for God to accept them.

Being good enough—being free from bad habits and bad behavior, earning enough "points" on the ledger of good behavior—is not what brings about a new spiritual birth in a person. Salvation is solely a matter of *believing in Jesus*. The repentance and change of behavior come later as the Holy Spirit prompts it, and also as the Holy Spirit helps a person to accomplish it! We will discuss this further in another lesson, but it is vitally important for you at this point to come to this understanding: Nothing you do *apart from believing in Jesus Christ* causes you to be saved. When you believe, the Spirit enters into you and causes your old sin nature to be transformed into a new nature that is in the likeness of God. The transformation of your spirit is a sovereign work of God; you cannot do it on your own, achieve it through your will or behavior, or force it to happen by any other means than believing.

• *What new insights do you have into the promises that God has made regarding your salvation?*

_____

_____

- *In your life, have you ever had an experience in which you repented (changed your mind) about a behavior and attempted then to change that behavior, only to fall back into an old pattern? How did you feel? What did you do?*

_____

_____

What the Word Says	What the Word Says to Me
For by grace you have been saved through faith, and that not of yourselves; it is the gift of God, not of works, lest anyone should boast (Eph. 2:8–9).	_____ _____ _____ _____ _____
When the kindness and the love of God our Savior toward man appeared, not by works of righteousness which we have done, but according to His mercy He saved us, through the washing of regeneration and renewing of the Holy Spirit, whom He poured out on us abundantly through Jesus Christ our Savior, that having been justified by His grace we should become heirs according to the hope of eternal life (Titus 3:4–7).	_____ _____ _____ _____ _____ _____ _____ _____ _____ _____ _____ _____

How Does This Relate to Eternal Security?

If you believe that your salvation came about by anything other than simply believing in what Jesus Christ did for you on the cross, then you believe that your salvation was in some way related to your own will and to your own works. If you believe that your salvation is related to your will and your works, then you will believe that your will and your works can in some way "undo" or negate your salvation.

On the other hand, if you believe that your salvation was based solely on what Jesus did for you and what the Holy Spirit has done in you, then you believe that your salvation was a sovereign work of God. Your part was simply to believe and receive what *God* provided and what *God* promised. The person who believes this must therefore conclude that since he did absolutely *nothing* to transform his old sin nature into a new spiritual nature, he cannot do anything to cause his new spiritual nature to revert to his old nature.

The critical questions are these:

- *Have you believed in Jesus as the sole, substitutionary, atoning sacrifice for your sin nature?*
- *Have you received the Holy Spirit of God into your life?*
- *Has the Holy Spirit transformed you and caused your spirit to be "reborn"?*

If you cannot answer "yes" with full assurance today, then I invite you to look upon the death of Jesus and to *believe* in Him today. Receive Him as your Savior.

You may want to pray this prayer or a similar one. The words are not important. What is important is the intent of your heart—to *believe in and receive* Jesus as Savior.

> I acknowledge to You, God, that I have a sin nature. No matter what I do or try, I cannot change this nature on my own. I acknowledge that my sin nature has separated me from You. Today, I look upon the cross on which Jesus Christ shed His blood, and I believe that Jesus is the provision that You have made for me to come into a right relationship with You. I believe that Jesus is the substitutionary, atoning sacrifice for *my* sin nature. I acknowledge Him as my Savior. And I receive, as an act of my believing, the promises that You have made: I receive Your promise of everlasting life. I receive Your promise that my spirit will be "reborn" by the Holy Spirit and that the Holy Spirit from this moment on will be resident in me to transform my nature and help me to live out a new life that is in full relationship with You and in full agreement with Your commandments. Thank You for sending

Jesus to die in my place. Thank You for loving me enough to want to live with me forever. I believe that from this day forward, and throughout all eternity, what Jesus has done for me is sufficient for me to be fully acceptable to You as Your child and Your heir of all heavenly promises.

• *In what ways are you feeling challenged in your spirit today?*

_____

_____

• *In what ways are you feeling challenged to change your thinking regarding your salvation?*

_____

_____

• *What new insights do you have into eternal security?*

_____

_____

WHY IT IS IMPORTANT FOR YOU TO BELIEVE IN ETERNAL SECURITY

A number of Christians seem to believe that it doesn't really matter whether a person believes in the position of eternal security or believes that a person can fall from grace. In my opinion, a person's belief on this issue is vitally important for several reasons, which we will cover in this lesson.

Knowing You Are Saved

First, and perhaps foremost, is the issue of whether a person can *know* that he or she is saved. The person who doesn't know with certainty that he is saved eternally is a person who frequently wonders if he is saved at all!

A significant number of Christians seem to wonder if they have already lost their salvation and don't know it. They say, "Oh, I know

I was saved 'back then,' but I've sinned so much since then that I'm not really certain that I'm still saved." Such a person very likely believes that he was saved by something other than believing, and therefore, there is something that he can do to "undo" his salvation. Implicit in this line of questioning is a question about whether *any* person can ever know with certainty whether he is saved or lost.

Jesus said that we *can* know. In the Gospel of John we read:

> But he who enters by the door is the shepherd of the sheep. To him the doorkeeper opens, and the sheep hear his voice; and he calls his own sheep by name and leads them out. And when he brings out his own sheep, he goes before them; and the sheep follow him, for they know his voice. Yet they will by no means follow a stranger, but will flee from him, for they do not know the voice of strangers. . . . Other sheep I have which are not of this fold; them also I must bring, and they will hear My voice; and there will be one flock and one shepherd (John 10:2–5, 16).

The inner witness of the Holy Spirit will always assure the genuinely born-again person that he or she *is* a forgiven child of God, in right standing with the Father.

The person who does not believe in the eternal security of his salvation is a person who not only has doubts about salvation but also has a certain amount of doubt about God, and especially about God's love, mercy, and ability to forgive. God desires that you *know* you are eternally secure and that you believe He is a loving, forgiving God whose mercy is without end. (See Lam. 3:22–24.)

- *In your life, have you ever questioned God's ability to extend mercy, love, or forgiveness to you or to someone you regard as a "repeat" sinner? Is your questioning related to your understanding about God's ability to save definitively and eternally?*

What the Word Says	What the Word Says to Me
It is the Spirit who bears witness, because the Spirit is truth (1 John 5:6).	------------------------------ ------------------------------ ------------------------------
There are three that bear witness on earth: the Spirit, the water, and the blood; and these three agree as one. If we receive the witness of men, the witness of God is greater; for this is the witness of God which He has testified of His Son. He who believes in the Son of God has the witness in himself. . . . These things I have written to you who believe in the name of the Son of God, that you may know that you have eternal life, and that you may continue to believe in the name of the Son of God (1 John 5:8–10, 13).	------------------------------ ------------------------------ ------------------------------ ------------------------------ ------------------------------ ------------------------------ ------------------------------ ------------------------------ ------------------------------ ------------------------------ ------------------------------ ------------------------------ ------------------------------ ------------------------------ ------------------------------ ------------------------------
Through the LORD's mercies we are not consumed, Because His compassions fail not. They are new every morning; Great is Your faithfulness. "The LORD is my portion," says my soul, "Therefore I hope in Him!" (Lam. 3:22–24).	------------------------------ ------------------------------ ------------------------------ ------------------------------ ------------------------------ ------------------------------ ------------------------------

For How Long Are You Saved?

Those who believe that salvation is a temporary thing—that it can come and go, and come and go again, repeatedly—must answer the question, "For how long, then, is a person saved?"

As Long as We Don't Sin?

Is a person saved only as long as he or she doesn't sin? Surely not, since none of us can live in our earthly bodies without being subject to temptation and to sin—willfully or instinctively, engaging in overt acts of sin (commission) as well as acts of neglect in doing the things we should do (omission). Paul made it very clear that "all have sinned," and although the Holy Spirit is resident within us to help us withstand temptation and to avoid sin, we remain fleshly beings who often do impulsively and reactively what we don't want to do deep in our hearts or what we wouldn't do if we took time to think about our actions. Paul wrote about this to the Romans:

> For I delight in the law of God according to the inward man. But I see another law in my members, warring against the law of my mind, and bringing me into captivity to the law of sin which is in my members. O wretched man that I am! Who will deliver me from this body of death? I thank God— through Jesus Christ our Lord! So then, with the mind I myself serve the law of God, but with the flesh the law of sin (Rom. 7:22–25).

• *Have you ever experienced such a "warring" between your mind and flesh? What did you do? How did God help you with this?*

_____

_____

If our salvation is only good as long as we remain sinless in our thoughts, words, and deeds, then certainly no person could be saved unless he or she died the very second that person said "Amen" to a prayer seeking God's forgiveness! If a temporary or fleeting salvation were God's will, certainly a merciful and loving God would then strike us dead the minute we accepted Jesus Christ as our Savior so that we might never "lose" His provision of forgiveness and a changed nature.

The fact is, we are all going to sin after we are saved. We don't want to sin, nevertheless we do. We live in fallen bodies, in a fallen world, and we are not yet made perfect in Christ. Each of us will make mistakes, even though it is our hearts' desire that we be perfect in Christ Jesus and obey God in all ways. It simply is not possible for any person to live an error-free, mistake-free, sin-free life every minute of every day.

The grace of God is all about God extending forgiveness to us even when we sin and fall short of God's perfect plan. (See Rom. 3:23 and 5:8.)

This inevitability that we will sin after salvation should not be taken as an excuse for sin, as a means of attempting to justify sin, or as a license to sin! *The person who truly knows Jesus as Savior and who has been born again will not want to sin and will sorrow at the thought that he has sinned.*

Neither does the inevitability that we will sin after our salvation keep us from experiencing the consequences of the sin we commit. We are very unwise to think we can say about our favorite sins, "Well, that's just the way I am. God knows that, so God won't punish me when I sin. I can't help myself." The fact is, you *can* help yourself! You can ask the Holy Spirit to help you withstand that particular temptation that seems to hound you. You can rely upon the Holy Spirit to give you the strength and courage you need to live a pure life. You can remain sensitive to the Holy Spirit's direction and to the Holy Spirit's conviction of sin. God has given you a will in which to say "no" to sin and "yes" to the Holy Spirit. It is within your capacity to be transformed so that you no longer have a desire to sin, so that you feel uncomfortable when you are around sin and repulsed at a discovery that you have sinned. Rather than say, "I can't help myself," we should be quick to say, "The Lord will help me" and quick to pray, "Lord, help me!" We must trust Christ in us to do for us what we cannot do ourselves. (See Phil. 4:13.)

Our response to God's grace must never be to take it for granted, but rather to thank and praise God that He is merciful toward us, patient with us, and faithful to us.

What the Word Says

My little children, these things I write to you, so that you may not

What the Word Says to Me

----

sin. And if anyone sins, we have an
Advocate with the Father, Jesus
Christ the righteous. And He
Himself is the propitiation for our
sins, and not for ours only but also
for the whole world (1 John
2:1–2).

I can do all things through Christ
who strengthens me (Phil. 4:13).

How Many Times?

How many times does Jesus have to die? How many times can
a person be born again? The answer surely should be immediate
in every Christian's mind for both of these questions: "Only once!"

The apostle Paul wrote regarding the death of Jesus on the cross,
"The death that He died, He died to sin once for all" (Rom. 6:10).
Yet those who believe that they can "lose" what Christ obtained
for them on the cross seem to put themselves into a position of cru-
cifying Christ again and again. They act as if the death of Jesus were
not sufficient the first time they went to the foot of the cross to look
upon Him and believe; therefore, they go again and again.

Just as Christ's death on the cross was definitive, so the work that
the Holy Spirit performs in bringing about a new spiritual "birth"
to the person who believes in Jesus as Savior is definitive. Another
way of asking this same question would be, "How many times does
the Holy Spirit 'rebirth' a person?" Only once! Just as a person cannot physically return to the womb after being born, so a person
cannot spiritually undo a new-birth experience once he or she has
been born again by the power of the Holy Spirit.

There is simply no such thing as a genuine expression of belief
in Jesus Christ *not* resulting in a new-birth spiritually. The person
who truly, humbly, and honestly accepts Jesus Christ as Savior *is*
born again.

Furthermore, the Spirit of God—once He has taken up resi-
dence in a person's spirit—does not die and does not leave. You
cannot "kill" the Holy Spirit within you, regardless of what you do!
You simply do not have that power over sovereign, almighty, omnipo-

tent, *omnipresent* God. God dwells where God chooses to dwell, and God chooses to dwell within the hearts and minds of those who have declared belief in His Son, Jesus Christ.

Wherever the Holy Spirit dwells, He brings life eternal because His own life is eternal. When the Holy Spirit dwells in your spirit, He brings His eternal life to your spirit. He does not depart, now or forever. (See Rom. 8:9–11.)

What the Word Says	What the Word Says to Me
You are not in the flesh but in the Spirit, if indeed the Spirit of God dwells in you. Now if anyone does not have the Spirit of Christ, he is not His. And if Christ is in you, the body is dead because of sin, but the Spirit is life because of righteousness. But if the Spirit of Him who raised Jesus from the dead dwells in you, He who raised Christ from the dead will also give life to your mortal bodies through His Spirit who dwells in you (Rom. 8:9–11).	_____ _____ _____ _____ _____ _____ _____ _____ _____ _____ _____ _____

• *How do you feel about the fact that you cannot evict the Holy Spirit from your heart?*

_____

_____

Was Christ's Death Sufficient?

Those who believe they can fall from grace cite their ongoing sin as the means by which they fall. Questions naturally arise:

• How much sin?
• How frequent a sin?
• How long is God's patience before He negates salvation in a person on account of their continued sin?

These questions have no answer in Scripture because they are the wrong questions to be asking! The fact is, once you have accepted Jesus Christ as your Savior, your sin cannot undo your salvation. You simply cannot "evict" the Holy Spirit from a heart He has chosen to indwell.

To say that you can negate your salvation by your sin is to say that Christ's death on the cross was not sufficient for your salvation in the first place. It is to say that something else had to be done to win or earn salvation—in essence, a person had to believe in Jesus Christ as the one, true, substitutionary, and atoning sacrifice *and then continue to live a sin-free life.* At no time is this requirement set forth in the Bible.

Christ's death was sufficient to pay your sin debt in *full.* Jesus paid it *all.* To believe otherwise is to hold the position that in some way Jesus' shed blood was an inadequate price for your eternal life. No person in his right mind would go to the bank to make a payment on a loan, discover that a benefactor had paid the loan in full, and then argue with the teller that even though the debt papers were stamped "Paid in Full," he still wanted to continue to make payments! To the contrary, such a person is likely to go running and skipping from that bank, shouting, "It's paid! It's paid!"

The same holds for our salvation. Jesus paid it all. When we think that there is *anything* we must do—or even *can* do—to add to the security of our salvation, we are attempting to pay for something that has already been purchased and given to us as a free gift motivated by God's love and mercy.

Why do people continue to try to pay for the free salvation Jesus has granted to them? I believe the main reason is pride. People want to think they have deserved or earned anything they have. We are reluctant receivers. Nevertheless, a "receiver" is precisely the position we are in. Our response should be thanksgiving and praise!

Is it "cheap salvation" because all that is required of us is our belief and our receiving of what is offered to us as a free gift of God? No! Our salvation cost Jesus' life, and there was nothing "cheap" about that! Our salvation is expensive salvation, but it is salvation that is offered to us as a precious, highly valuable, to-be-treasured gift. We must never take our salvation lightly. At the same time, there is nothing we can do to deserve or to win our salvation as an award or reward.

The simple truth is this: you can't pay for your salvation, either before or after you receive it. Christ already paid for it.

What the Word Says	What the Word Says to Me
A man is not justified by the works of the law but by faith in Jesus Christ, even we have believed in Christ Jesus, that we might be justified by faith in Christ and not by the works of the law; for by the works of the law no flesh shall be justified (Gal. 2:16).	------------------------------
I have been crucified with Christ; it is no longer I who live, but Christ lives in me; and the life which I now live in the flesh I live by faith in the Son of God, who loved me and gave Himself for me. I do not set aside the grace of God; for if righteousness comes through the law, then Christ died in vain (Gal. 2:20–21).	------------------------------
Thanks be to God for His indescribable gift! (2 Cor. 9:15).	------------------------------
To each one of us grace was given according to the measure of Christ's gift (Eph. 4:7).	------------------------------

The Impact on Your Daily Life

What you believe about eternal security has a direct bearing on your daily life. If you believe that your salvation can be "lost," then you will take one of two positions:

1. You will be in a state of constantly striving to "keep" your salvation, which often ends in great anxiety or perhaps a false sense of righteousness, or
2. You will be in a state of feeling the futility of your efforts—a feeling of frustration and despair—because eventually you will be forced to face the fact that you have not led a sin-free life since you believed in Christ, and you will not be able to lead such a life in the future.

Neither of these states is a good one!

- *In your life, have you ever found yourself striving to be perfect in order to maintain your relationship with God—striving to the point of frustration, exhaustion, or discouragement?*

_____

_____

- *How does it feel to face the fact that even though you have believed in Christ, you have not continued to live a sin-free life? What do you do with those feelings?*

_____

_____

The person who continues to strive to in some way earn or "secure" his salvation is a person who eventually will lose his joy. He also may eventually lose his hope. The person who feels that he simply cannot maintain a sin-free life will eventually question God's desire to forgive. He will say to himself, "I've sinned so often, and repented so often, and been saved so often, and then fallen away so often, God is probably sick and tired of me. Surely He won't continue to forgive me." Never attribute to God your own inability or your own lack of patience! God is a long-suffering God. An even deeper issue, however, is that God does not desire that you live in this state. He wants you to know that He has forgiven you, you are born again, and He is working within you to bring about the complete transformation of your life into the fullness of the stature of Christ Jesus. God will deal with your sin and use it to train you in the ways of righteousness, but He does not strip away your salvation or your heavenly home in the process!

The Impact on Your Witness

Not only does a belief that you can fall from God's grace impact your daily life, but it impacts your witness for Jesus Christ. If you believe you can lose your salvation, what is it that you say to another person to convince him or her to be born again? If you believe you are only saved as long as you remain sin-free, what kind of "blessed assurance" is it that you offer to another person in Christ Jesus?

What kind of offer of forgiveness is it if you say to another person, "Well, I'll forgive you for what you did to me, but only if you never sin again against me or anybody else"?

That certainly isn't the offer that God makes to us! God tacks on no ifs, ands, buts, or any other kind of qualifier to the offer of forgiveness and salvation that He extends to us through Christ Jesus. Our heavenly Father did not say, "If you believe in Jesus *and* . . ." Our belief in Jesus was, is, and always will be sufficient. That's the good news! To add anything to God's offer of salvation is to add a bit of bad news to God's good news.

Those who believe a person can fall from grace often have a very difficult time motivating themselves to witness actively about Jesus Christ for the simple reason that they don't truly believe that a person can come to Christ without some kind of ongoing struggle in their lives. Any salesman knows that it is extremely difficult to motivate himself to make sales calls if he knows he has a flawed or bad product to sell. The same is true for the gospel. Either it is the supremely good news of eternal salvation, or it is a flawed provision that requires the futile efforts of man.

Others witness about Christ in hopes that their witness is a "good work" that will secure their salvation by offsetting some of their own sins. Can you see the error in that? Not only is their motivation ill-founded, but eventually they will despair in their attempts at witnessing and become discouraged.

In sharp contrast, those who believe they are eternally secure tend to have an exuberance in witnessing. They are offering a glorious salvation, a truly wonderful gift of God to the sinner. They know that it is Jesus who saves, the Holy Spirit who indwells, and that a person who has been saved becomes God's own child to train, nurture, and love forever.

What a tremendous future we have been given!

- *In your experience, have you found it difficult to witness to others about Jesus and about the need to be saved? Do you know why? Is it perhaps because of what you have believed about salvation?*

  _____

  _____

- *What new insights do you have into God's Word regarding eternal security?*

  _____

  _____

- *In what ways are you feeling challenged today regarding the eternally secure nature of your own salvation?*

  _____

  _____

LESSON 4

SEVEN REASONS FOR BELIEVING IN ETERNAL SECURITY: PART 1

Much concern is registered in our world regarding various types of security. We all long to be financially secure, to have our homes and other possessions remain secure against thieves and vandals, and to enjoy personal safety and security. Our spiritual security, however, is the most precious type of security we can know. If we have peace of mind knowing that our finances are in order, our homes and possessions are safe, our family members are safe, and we ourselves are safe . . . how much more peace can we enjoy by knowing that we are saved *forever* and a home is being prepared for us in eternity!

The Scriptures provide seven overriding reasons for believing in eternal security. We will deal with three of them in this lesson:

1. The omnipotence and omnipresence of God
2. The continuing intercession of Christ on our behalf
3. The prevailing love of Christ

God's Omnipotence and Omnipresence

The first great reason for believing in eternal security lies in the very nature of God. What we believe about our salvation is always directly or indirectly related to what we believe to be true about God.

Many people seem to think that God and the devil are on an equal plane—God is on the side of good, the devil is on the side of bad—and mankind is between the two, caught in something of a great tug-of-war between opposite but equal forces. That is *not* what the Bible teaches.

God is sovereign. He is the Almighty One, the King of the universe. The devil is totally subject to God's authority; he operates only within the boundaries that God defines. God is victor over the devil in any conflict.

The devil—once the archangel Lucifer—fell from God's presence in heaven through his rebellion and attempted overthrow of God's throne. The lie that the devil attempts to foist upon mankind is that man can also fall from God's presence any time man rebels or sins. While that is true for mankind as a whole—we are born with a sin nature because of the "fall" of Adam and Eve—that is *not* true for the person who has believed in Jesus Christ and received the gift of eternal life. Such a person is firmly established as being with God, in God, and inseparable from God. That person cannot fall away from God, nor can the devil snatch that person away from God in a tug-of-war contest.

Consider these unchanging attributes of God:

- God does not lie. His Word is true. The devil is the one who is a liar. (See John 8:44.)
- God cannot be defeated by the devil or by any human being. The devil is a defeated foe, eternally defeated by Jesus' death on the cross. (See 1 Cor. 15:57.)
- God does not change, regardless of how a human being may change. The devil is the one who appears in many guises. (See Heb. 13:8.)

- God cannot be avoided, escaped, or removed by any act or will of man. We can, however, resist the devil so that he will flee from us. (See James 4:7.)

God is supreme and infinite. The devil is subject to God and is finite.

These attributes of God's nature are especially important in the light of our *relationship* with God. Once we have believed in Jesus Christ and received Him as our Savior, we enter a lasting relationship with God. The shed blood of Jesus has qualified us fully for this relationship; God is the author of the relationship and His presence begins to abide with us in a way that transforms us. *We are eternally in His grip!* Nothing the devil can say or do alters our position or destroys our relationship with God.

The psalmist wrote about God, "The LORD is my shepherd; I shall not want" (Ps. 23:1). As a sheep of the Lord, David recognized that God provided for him rest, nourishment, guidance, protection, blessing, and a full restoration of soul. He concluded, "Surely goodness and mercy shall follow me all the days of my life; and I will dwell in the house of the LORD forever" (Ps. 23:6). At no time does the psalmist remotely indicate that his relationship with the Lord is tentative, subject to being broken, or that he can cease being a sheep in God's fold.

Jesus echoed this in saying, "I am the good shepherd" (John 10:11). Later in the Gospel of John, Jesus said as He prayed for His disciples:

> I have manifested Your name to the men whom You have given Me out of the world. They were Yours, You gave them to Me, and they have kept Your word. Now they have known that all things which You have given Me are from You. For I have given to them the words which You have given Me; and they have received them, and have known surely that I came forth from You; and they have believed that You sent Me. I pray for them. I do not pray for the world but for those whom You have given Me, for they are Yours. And all Mine are Yours, and Yours are Mine, and I am glorified in them. . . . Keep through Your name those whom You have given Me,

that they may be one as We are. While I was with them in
the world, I kept them in Your name. Those whom You gave
Me I have kept; and none of them is lost except the son of
perdition, that the Scripture might be fulfilled. . . . I do
not pray for these alone, but also for those who will believe
in Me through their word; that they all may be one, as You,
Father, are in Me, and I in You; that they also may be one
in Us, that the world may believe that You sent Me (John
17:6–12, 20–21).

• *What new insights do you have into this passage of Scripture?*

_____

_____

Note that Jesus said that He hasn't lost a single disciple that the
Father gave to Him. Neither has the Father ever lost a soul that has
believed in Jesus Christ. When we are reunited to God through the
blood of Jesus Christ, we are inseparable from God. We become
"one" with Him. We cannot be snatched or pried away from Him.
His omnipotence (all powerful nature) assures that no power can
rip us away from His love and care.

What the Word Says

You have a mighty arm;
Strong is Your hand, and high is
Your right hand.
Righteousness and justice are the
foundation of Your throne;
Mercy and truth go before Your
face.
Blessed are the people who know
the joyful sound!
They walk, O LORD, in the light of
Your countenance.
In Your name they rejoice all day
long,
And in Your righteousness they

What the Word Says to Me

----

are exalted.
For You are the glory of their
strength,
And in Your favor our horn is
exalted.
For our shield belongs to the
LORD (Ps. 89:13–18).

God is our refuge and strength,
A very present help in trouble. . . .
God is in the midst of her, she
shall not be moved (Ps. 46:1, 5).

[Jesus said,] "All authority has
been given to Me in heaven and
on earth. . . . And lo, I am with
you always" (Matt. 28:18, 20).

If God is for us, who can be
against us? (Rom. 8:31).

Our eternal security lies in the fact that God is undefeatable and always present. He knows all, sees all, and is victorious over all. Nothing can take Him by surprise or catch Him off guard. He cannot be tricked, manipulated, or conned. The devil and all the demons of hell cannot steal you away from His eternal grasp.

- *How do you feel knowing that the devil simply cannot "steal" you away from God?*

_____

_____

The Intercession of Christ for Us

In various places in the New Testament we read that Jesus Christ is presently seated at the right hand of God the Father, where He is interceding, mediating, or "advocating" for us. As you read the verses below, apply them to *yourself* and your salvation.

What the Word Says	What the Word Says to Me
He is also able to save to the uttermost those who come to God through Him, since He always lives to make intercession for them (Heb. 7:25).	_____ _____ _____ _____ _____
For Christ has not entered the holy places made with hands . . . but into heaven itself, now to appear in the presence of God for us (Heb. 9:24).	_____ _____ _____ _____ _____
It is God who justifies. . . . It is Christ who died, . . . who is even at the right hand of God, who also makes intercession for us (Rom. 8:33–34).	_____ _____ _____ _____ _____
We have an Advocate with the Father, Jesus Christ the righteous (1 John 2:1).	_____ _____ _____

What is it that Jesus is praying for us in heaven? Very likely it is the same prayer we find in John 17:15–19, 24:

> I do not pray that You should take them out of the world, but that You should keep them from the evil one. They are not of the world, just as I am not of the world. Sanctify them by Your truth. Your word is truth. As You sent Me into the world, I also have sent them into the world. And for their sakes I sanctify Myself, that they also may be sanctified by the truth. . . . Father, I desire that they also whom You gave Me may be with Me where I am, that they may behold My glory which You have given Me; for You loved Me before the foundation of the world.

In summary, Jesus is praying that we will be delivered from evil, be victorious witnesses to the gospel of Jesus Christ, and behold the glory of Jesus. What a wonderful prayer is being made on your behalf every moment since you believed on Jesus Christ and received Him as your Savior! Do you think that God the Father will fail to answer the prayer of His Son—even for an instant?

Jesus' prayer for us is about our relationship with Him and with the Father. We certainly can err or sin by our will, but Jesus' intercession for us will then bring about our chastening so that our eternal relationship with the Father might become even stronger and more intimate. Jesus' prayer attests to the permanence of our relationship "in God" so that we become "one" with Him and with Christ. With Jesus praying this about our relationship with God—which He purchased with His own blood—how dare we believe that we can in any way negate, abolish, or supersede His prayer.

- *How do you feel knowing that Jesus is continually praying for you in heaven at the right hand of the Father?*

_____

_____

The Prevailing Love of Christ

One of the most stirring and comforting passages of the entire New Testament is Romans 8:35–39:

Who shall separate us from the love of Christ? Shall tribulation, or distress, or persecution, or famine, or nakedness, or peril, or sword? As it is written:
"For Your sake we are killed all day long;
We are accounted as sheep for the slaughter."
Yet in all these things we are more than conquerors through Him who loved us. For I am persuaded that neither death nor life, nor angels nor principalities nor powers, nor things present nor things to come, nor height nor depth, nor any other created thing, shall be able to separate us from the love of God which is in Christ Jesus our Lord.

- *What new insights do you have into this passage of Scripture?*

_____

_____

This statement by Paul is made just after he told the Romans, "We know that all things work together for good to those who love God, to those who are the called according to His purpose. For whom He foreknew, He also predestined to be conformed to the image of His Son, that He might be the firstborn among many brethren. Moreover whom He predestined, these He also called; whom He called, these He also justified; and whom He justified, these He also glorified" (Rom. 8:28–30).

Paul's statement, therefore, about the prevailing reach of Christ's love is for those who are:

- *The beloved who have been called according to God's purpose*—those who have believed in Jesus and received God's gift of forgiveness and everlasting life.
- *The justified*—those who are no longer guilty in their sins but have been declared righteous because of their belief in Jesus, who paid their sin debt in full.
- *The glorified*—those who will assuredly witness and partake of Christ's eternal glory, bound and identified with Him so that whatever glory Christ receives, He receives because of what He has done for us, and in turn, we reflect the glory of His nature in us.

Paul asks three questions related to our position in Christ's love:

1. Who can accuse us and make it stick? (See Rom. 8:33.)
2. Who can condemn us and make us guilty? (See Rom. 8:34.)
3. Who can separate us from Christ? (See Rom. 8:35.)

The answer to these three questions is the same: nothing and nobody! No *event* or *state of being* can destroy the prevailing power of Christ's love in our lives. There is *no person or demonic power* that can destroy Christ's love for us. There is no *time* in which we are separated from His love. There is *nothing in heaven or hell* that can pry us from His love!

Christ's love for us is a shield that cannot be penetrated, removed, or deactivated!

• *What new insights do you have into Romans 8:28–30?*

_____

_____

If there were ever a person who would have been deemed worthy in the eyes of man to be estranged from Christ or removed from Christ's love, it would have been Peter, who denied knowing Jesus three times at the most stressful and consequential period of Jesus' earthly life. Yet Jesus appeared to Peter after the Resurrection to ask Peter three times (the same number of times Peter had denied Him): Do you love Me? (See John 21:15–19.) Jesus gave Peter a full opportunity to reestablish the truth of his love for the Lord. What was *never* in question, however, was Jesus' love for Peter! That remained constant and prevailing—it was not even dented by what Peter had done or failed to do.

Very often when we doubt that God can love us, what we are really doubting is ourselves—that we are worthy of God's love. God is the One who declares that we are worthy to love. He is the One who found us so worthy to love that He sent His only begotten Son, Jesus Christ, to die on a cross in our place. We do not determine our worthiness; God does! And He says to each of us, "I love you with an immeasurable, lasting love. My love motivates My mercy, My forgiveness, and My steadfast faithfulness." It is up to us to receive what God gives. As John wrote, "We love Him because He first loved us" (1 John 4:19).

What should be our response to Christ's prevailing love, which keeps us in an inseparable relationship with Him? To love Him back! To thank and praise Him for His great love. And, as John also wrote, "to love one another" (1 John 4:11).

Paul wrote eloquently about love in 1 Corinthians 13. Very often we think of this chapter as pertaining only to human love—the love of one person for another person. At times we may think of it as relating to our love for God. As you read through the following verses, I encourage you to think in terms of God loving *you*. The love we are capable of having for others is born first of God's great love for us. And, oh, how He does love us!

What the Word Says

In this is love, not that we loved God, but that He loved us and sent His Son to be the propitiation for our sins. Beloved, if God so loved us, we also ought to love one another (1 John 4:10–11).

Love suffers long and is kind; love . . . does not behave rudely . . . is not provoked, thinks no evil; does not rejoice in iniquity, but rejoices in the truth; bears all things, believes all things, hopes all things, endures all things. Love never fails (1 Cor. 13:4–8).

What the Word Says to Me

• *In your life, have you truly experienced the love of God? What new insights do you have into God's love for you?*

_____

_____

• *In what ways are you feeling challenged today regarding the eternal security of your soul in Christ Jesus?*

_____

_____

SEVEN REASONS FOR BELIEVING IN ETERNAL SECURITY: PART 2

The apostle Peter wrote, "Always be ready to give a defense to everyone who asks you a reason for the hope that is in you" (1 Peter 3:15). Certainly nothing gives a person more cause for hope than to know that he or she is saved from the consequences of their sin nature by believing in Jesus Christ, and that they have an everlasting relationship with God and a home in heaven. What reasons might we give for having such a hope?

In the last lesson, we covered three reasons for believing in eternal security. In this lesson, we will deal with four additional reasons:

1. God's eternal purpose for us
2. The irreversible nature of our new life in Christ
3. The binding nature of the Holy Spirit's "seal" on our lives
4. The faithfulness of God

God's Eternal Purpose for Us

In the last lesson we cited Paul's encouraging words to the Romans: "For whom He foreknew, He also predestined to be conformed to the image of His Son, that He might be the firstborn among many brethren. Moreover whom He predestined, these He also called; whom He called, these He also justified; and whom He justified, these He also glorified" (Rom. 8:29–30).

I want to call your attention to two main things about this brief passage. *First, God's purpose for you is a total "conformation" to the image of His Son, Jesus Christ.* To be conformed to something is to become *like* it in all essential factors. God's purpose for each of us is that we *talk* like Jesus—we say what Jesus would say if He were in whatever situation we happen to find ourselves. We *respond* like Jesus—we do what He would do if He were facing our particular circumstances or decisions. We *act boldly with love and power* in any situation where we find need, sickness, or pain.

Jesus sent out His disciples, telling them, "As you go, preach, saying, 'The kingdom of heaven is at hand.' Heal the sick, cleanse the lepers, raise the dead, cast out demons. Freely you have received, freely give" (Matt. 10:7–8). The disciples were given power over unclean spirits, to cast them out, and to heal all kinds of sickness and all kinds of disease. (See Matt. 10:1.) This is a portrait of conformation. The disciples were conformed to the nature and the likeness of Jesus. What they did, we are expected to continue to do today as we are conformed to Him through the power of the Holy Spirit. The Holy Spirit has been given to all who believe in Jesus and receive Him as Savior so that we might *be* Christ's ambassadors in our world today.

- *How do you feel about being conformed to the image of Christ Jesus?*

_____

_____

Second, God's conformation process has four progressive and irreversible stages: predestined, called, justified, and glorified. Our conformation begins with the fact that God has predestined us for this process. God's very purpose for your creation, birth, and ongoing life on this earth is so that He might conform you into the nature of Christ and live with you forever. He called you, and in hearing the call of God, you came to accept Jesus as your Savior. In accepting Jesus, you were justified by God so that you were no longer held bound by your sin nature, but rather, you received the very spirit of Christ Jesus into your life. In being justified, you are in the process of being glorified. These four stages proceed naturally and normally without variation in the life of every person who comes to believe in Jesus Christ as Savior. There are no variations on this theme, no alternate routes, no different processes. You were predestined to be called; you were called in order to be justified; you were justified to be glorified.

It is folly to think it remotely possible that we can reverse this God-ordained process. You cannot go from being justified back to being uncalled!

• *In your life, can you see how these stages have progressed?*

_____

_____

The third thing I want you to note in this passage is that all four words associated with this conformation process are in the past tense. Most of us tend to think that perhaps we will be glorified one day, and those who believe it is possible to fall from grace say that we *might* be glorified if we continue to live the right way. Paul writes about our glorification as an accomplished fact. It's a "done deal." Since the progression is irreversible, every believer *will* be glorified.

Once you enter God's conformation process through believing in Jesus Christ, nothing you or anyone else can do will reverse that process or keep it from happening. God *will* justify and glorify you. The good work that has begun in you will continue and eventually be completed because the One doing the work is God! (See Heb. 12:2.)

What the Word Says	What the Word Says to Me
Looking unto Jesus, the author and finisher of our faith (Heb. 12:2).	------------------------------ ------------------------------ ------------------------------
I thank my God upon every remembrance of you, . . . being confident of this very thing, that He who has begun a good work in you will complete it until the day of Jesus Christ; . . . you all are partakers with me of grace (Phil. 1:3, 6, 7).	------------------------------ ------------------------------ ------------------------------ ------------------------------ ------------------------------ ------------------------------ ------------------------------

- *What new insights do you have regarding God's eternal purposes for you as a believer in Christ Jesus?*

_____

_____

An Irreversible New Nature

In an earlier lesson we asked the question, "How can a person who is born physically reenter the womb and become 'unborn'?" It isn't possible. Neither is it possible for a person who has been spiritually reborn to become "unborn." The image of being born anew spiritually is a strong one and one to which every person can relate. The irreversible nature of this condition, however, is frequently left untaught or unexplained. When a person is born physically, he enters a completely new dimension of being. He breathes in the atmosphere of the earth and from that moment on, he is dependent upon oxygen. He cannot live without oxygen for more than a few minutes. Thus, he can never return to an existence of living in the fluid of his mother's body.

This is also true for us spiritually. Once we have believed in Jesus Christ and received the salvation that Christ purchased for us on the cross, we are filled with the Spirit of God and we cannot undo that "new state" in which we find ourselves. From that moment on, we live and move and have our being in Christ Jesus. (See Acts 17:28.)

New Creatures

Two other statements that refer to an irreversible "state of being" are also used by New Testament writers. Paul wrote to the Corinthians that "if anyone is in Christ, he is a new creation; old things have passed away; behold, all things have become new" (2 Cor. 5:17).

The new creature we have become is incapable of thinking and responding as the old creature did. The Holy Spirit begins to prick the conscience of the believer so that suddenly, the person who has come to Christ sees life from a completely new perspective. Things that were not previously thought to be sins come to be seen as sins. It truly is as if scales have been dropped from our eyes and we are able to see God, ourselves, our relationship with God, and all of life from a new point of view. We can never go back to a state of "not knowing," "not seeing," or "not understanding" because the very Spirit of Truth is now resident in us. (See John 14:17.)

Adopted Sons and Daughters

A third word that relates to our new state of being in Christ Jesus is *adoption*. Paul wrote, "For as many as are led by the Spirit of God, these are sons of God. For you did not receive the spirit of bondage again to fear, but you received the Spirit of adoption by whom we cry out, 'Abba, Father'" (Rom. 8:14–15).

In the ancient world, the child who was adopted actually had more rights than a child born into a family. A father could give up his natural-born child to adoption, but a child once adopted could never be given up again. It was illegal to do so. A natural-born child could be expelled from the family, disowned, or denied. An adopted child, however, could not be dissociated from the father who had adopted him. Paul was well aware of the legal rights and ramifications of adoption when he wrote that believers in Christ Jesus are full partakers of "the adoption, the glory, the covenants, the giving of the law, the service of God, and the promises" once thought to be available only to the Jews (Rom. 9:4). Believers in Christ Jesus are not second-class members of the family of God but full sons and daughters of the Almighty! (See Gal. 4:4–7 and Eph. 1:3–5.)

Can a person who has been born become "unborn"? No.

Can a new creation be "unmade" and become an old creation? No.

Can a child adopted by God become "unadopted"? No.

Each of these word pictures alludes to an irreversible state of being. What God transforms cannot be "undone" or "untransformed." Having entered a new spiritual state, we are in that state throughout the rest of our lives and into eternity.

What the Word Says	What the Word Says to Me
For in Him we live and move and have our being (Acts 17:28).	------------------------------- -------------------------------
But God forbid that I should boast except in the cross of our Lord Jesus Christ, by whom the world has been crucified to me, and I to the world. For in Christ Jesus neither circumcision nor uncircumcision avails anything, but a new creation (Gal. 6:14–15).	------------------------------- ------------------------------- ------------------------------- ------------------------------- ------------------------------- ------------------------------- ------------------------------- -------------------------------
When the fullness of the time had come, God sent forth His Son, born of a woman, born under the law, to redeem those who were under the law, that we might receive the adoption as sons. And because you are sons, God has sent forth the Spirit of His Son into your hearts, crying out, "Abba, Father!" Therefore you are no longer a slave but a son, and if a son, then an heir of God through Christ (Gal. 4:4–7).	------------------------------- ------------------------------- ------------------------------- ------------------------------- ------------------------------- ------------------------------- ------------------------------- ------------------------------- ------------------------------- ------------------------------- ------------------------------- ------------------------------- -------------------------------
Blessed be the God and Father of our Lord Jesus Christ, who has	------------------------------- -------------------------------

blessed us with every spiritual
blessing in the heavenly places in
Christ, just as He chose us in Him
before the foundation of the
world, that we should be holy and
without blame before Him in love,
having predestined us to adoption
as sons by Jesus Christ to Himself, according to the good
pleasure of His will (Eph. 1:3–5).

The irreversible nature of our new lives as sons and daughters
of God is portrayed in the story told by Jesus about a loving father
and a prodigal son. (See Luke 15:11–32.) At no time in this story
do we find any indication that the prodigal son *ceased* to belong
to his father's family. Even though he went as far away from his
father as he could go, wasted his possessions and his inheritance,
and fell to a point of near starvation slopping pigs for a pagan, this
prodigal son was welcomed home by his father without recrimi-
nation, without any sign of rejection or alienation, and without any
condemnation. The prodigal son lost a great deal in his sin—he
surely lost, at least temporarily, his status, his health, and his possessions. But he did *not* lose his relationship with his father. He was
always his father's son, and the father moved quickly upon the boy's
return to restore to him the visible marks of sonship: sandals, a
cloak, and a ring.

The same is true for us—regardless of what we may do after
we become a child of God through Christ Jesus (see Eph. 1:5), we
do not lose our relationship with God. He remains our loving, forgiving heavenly Father, always available to us with open arms. We
are His children forever.

- *Read Luke 15:11–31. What new insights do you have into this
passage of Scripture about eternal security?*

The Sure Seal of the Holy Spirit

Paul wrote to the Ephesians that as believers, we have been "sealed with the Holy Spirit of promise, who is the guarantee of our inheritance until the redemption of the purchased possession, to the praise of His glory" (Eph. 1:13–14).

What does it mean to be "sealed"? In the ancient world, a seal upon an item meant two things. First, the item was linked to a specific owner. Seals bore markings that indicated to whom the object belonged, from whom it had been sent, or by whom it had been purchased. To be sealed by the Holy Spirit is an indication that we are now "owned" by God the Father for His purposes.

A seal also meant that an item was authentic. Seals were rarely forged because each seal was handmade, and therefore, variations were easily spotted. When we are sealed by the Holy Spirit, the Holy Spirit "authenticates" our conversion experience. The Holy Spirit becomes the witness to the fact that we have believed in Jesus. It is as if the Spirit Himself says, "Yea and amen" to our act of believing in and receiving Christ.

Once the Holy Spirit indwells us, the very presence of the Holy Spirit is a "living seal" that we are God's children, fully authentic as heirs of Christ. Nobody and nothing can undo the seal of the Holy Spirit in the life of a believer. As Paul wrote to the Corinthians, we are no longer our own. Our bodies are members of Christ's body. The spirit within us is Christ's Spirit. We belong to God. (See 1 Cor. 6:15, 17, 19–20.)

What the Word Says	What the Word Says to Me
Do you not know that your bodies are members of Christ? . . . He who is joined to the Lord is one spirit with Him. . . . Do you not know that your body is the temple of the Holy Spirit who is in you, whom you have from God, and you are not your own? For you were bought at a price; therefore	---------------------------- ---------------------------- ---------------------------- ---------------------------- ---------------------------- ---------------------------- ---------------------------- ----------------------------

glorify God in your body and in
your spirit, which are God's
(1 Cor. 6:15, 17, 19–20).

_____

_____

_____

Paul wrote to the Ephesians that the Holy Spirit is a seal "of promise." What is this promise? It is the promise of "the guarantee of our inheritance until the redemption of the purchased possession" (Eph. 1:13–14). In other words, the Holy Spirit seals us until the day when God greets us face-to-face in heaven and we are secure in His presence there forever. Our full redemption is accomplished the day we enter God's glory in heaven. Until then, the Holy Spirit is the firm "guarantee" that this redemption _will_ take place.

• _How do you feel knowing that your redemption is guaranteed?_

_____

_____

• _What new insights do you have into eternal security?_

_____

_____

God's Absolute Faithfulness

God does what God says He will do. At no time in the Scriptures do we find God failing to keep His word or fulfill His promises. Paul wrote about this to Timothy:

This is a faithful saying:
For if we died with Him,
_ we shall also live with Him._
If we endure,
_ we shall also reign with Him._
If we deny Him,
_ He also will deny us._
If we are faithless,
_ He remains faithful;_
He cannot deny Himself (2 Tim. 2:11–13).

God does not change. He is the same yesterday, today, and forever. (See Heb. 13:8.) In Him, there is no variance, no turning, no shadow. (See James 1:17.)

Furthermore, God does not play favorites or show partiality to one person over another. What He has said or promised to one, He says and promises to all. (See Acts 10:34.) His word bears no mark of hypocrisy. (See James 3:17.)

The unchanging, steadfast, absolute nature of God makes God utterly faithful and trustworthy. If God has said that we receive everlasting life when we believe in Jesus Christ, we can count on that being true! If God has extended the promise of eternal life to "whosoever believeth," then the promise is surely to all who believe! All of the promises and teachings that pertain to eternal security can be relied upon as *truth*.

Ultimately, we need no other reason to believe in eternal security than this: God said that He gives eternal life to those who believe in Jesus Christ. What God says, God does.

What the Word Says

I thank my God always concerning you for the grace of God which was given to you by Christ Jesus, that you were enriched in every thing by Him . . . who will also confirm you to the end, that you may be blameless in the day of our Lord Jesus Christ. God is faithful, by whom you were called into the fellowship of His Son, Jesus Christ our Lord (1 Cor. 1:4–5, 8–9).

The Lord is faithful, who will establish you and guard you from the evil one (2 Thess. 3:3).

Now may the God of peace Himself sanctify you completely; and

What the Word Says to Me

----

may your whole spirit, soul, and
body be preserved blameless at
the coming of our Lord Jesus
Christ. He who calls you is faithful, who also will do it (1 Thess.
5:23–24).

Now I saw heaven opened, and
behold, a white horse. And He
who sat on him was called Faithful and True. . . . And He has on
His robe and on His thigh a
name written: KING OF
KINGS AND LORD OF
LORDS (Rev. 19:11, 16).

- *What new insights do you have into eternal security?*

- *In what ways are you feeling challenged regarding the eternally
  secure nature of your salvation?*

LESSON 6

SOLEMN WARNINGS: PART 1

In the next two lessons, we are going to deal with some of the arguments that are put forward by those who hold to the belief that it is possible to "fall from grace"—which is to "lose" one's salvation or to backslide spiritually to the point of needing to be "saved again."

We need to recognize as we begin this portion of our study that the devil is the "accuser of our brethren" (Rev. 12:10). The devil accuses believers as well as unbelievers. In fact, John wrote that he accuses the brethren "before God day and night."

Part of the devil's accusation to believers is that they are *not* born again and that they are separated from God by their sin. Certainly the devil knows that if he can keep Christians preoccupied with their own salvation, they will be far less effective in evangelism and other types of ministry. If the devil can plant doubts in a believer's mind regarding his or her eternal destiny, he can readily plant doubts about the nature of God, the nature of the relationship God desires with man, and the nature of the Holy Spirit's work within us.

Why Do We Doubt?

As we begin this portion of our study, we also must ask ourselves: "Why is it that believers doubt they are eternally secure in Christ

Jesus?" The devil tempts us to doubt, but why is it that we yield to his temptation?

I believe there are two reasons: First, we continue to sin after we are saved and many Christians have not been taught properly regarding the difference between a sin nature (which separates man from God) and sinful acts (which can be committed by both believers and nonbelievers). We will discuss sin and its consequences in a later chapter.

Second, many Christians have been taught certain passages of Scripture that seem to say, on the surface, that a person can "lose" his salvation. When one studies these passages *completely, in context,* and *in the full depth of their meaning in comparison to other similar teachings on the same subject,* a picture emerges that is strongly in support of eternal security. We will focus on these passages in the next two lessons so that you might not only understand the basis on which some believe we can fall from grace, but so that you also will know how to respond to those who hold that position.

Rather than regard these Scripture passages as supporting falling from grace, I believe these passages serve as "solemn warnings" to the church. Their purpose is not to pass judgment or issue condemnation, but rather to teach, warn, and admonish believers on very particular issues. As you approach these passages, I encourage you to see them as warnings that the Holy Spirit intends for believers to take very seriously, but always within the broader context of God's grace and mercy.

"Fallen from Grace"

Paul wrote to the Galatians:

> Stand fast therefore in the liberty by which Christ has made us free, and do not be entangled again with a yoke of bondage. Indeed I, Paul, say to you that if you become circumcised, Christ will profit you nothing. And I testify again to every man who becomes circumcised that he is a debtor to keep the whole law. You have become estranged from Christ, you who attempt to be justified by law; you have fallen from grace. For we through the Spirit eagerly wait for

the hope of righteousness by faith. For in Christ Jesus neither circumcision nor uncircumcision avails anything, but
faith working through love (Gal. 5:1–6).

This passage is often the basis on which people believe in the
possibility of falling from grace since it uses the very phrase, "fallen
from grace." We must be very careful to read this passage in the
context of the entire book of Galatians, and to have a clear understanding of the audience to whom Paul was writing, if we are to
understand fully its meaning.

Paul was writing primarily to churches that he founded on his
missionary journeys. Some of the members of these churches were
Jewish Christians—people who had been born Jewish and had
grown up with Jewish traditions, and who since had heard and
received the gospel of Jesus Christ. Others were Gentiles who had
come into the church. Both Jews and Christians were influenced
by the Greek and Roman cultures, a fact that caused confusion in
many of the new converts.

After their conversion to Christ, the Galatians were visited by
people called "Judaizers," those who taught that if a Jew was going
to be a Christian, he still had to keep all of the Law of Moses. Furthermore, the Judaizers taught the Gentiles who had come to Christ
that they needed to be circumcised and to follow all of the Law
of Moses, as well as all the oral rabbinical laws and traditions of
Judaism. To the Judaizers, a person could not be a Christian without also becoming a full-fledged Jew.

Paul disagreed strongly with the Judaizers. He wrote to the Galatians for the purpose of saying very directly to them, "If you go
back to the old way of keeping the Law and assuming that you are
in right standing with God because you keep the Law, you have
totally negated what Christ did on the cross. If you go back,
you will render Christ's death on the cross as being of no bene-
fit to you." Another way of saying this would have been, "If you
return to the Law as your means of salvation, why have Christ?
Christ fulfilled the Law. He embodied the Law. To believe in
Christ is to believe in something that supersedes the old Law.
Why live in the bondage of the Law, which does nothing but point

out to you that you are a sinner in need of salvation, when you can live in the freedom of forgiveness made possible by Jesus Christ?"

Paul was a strong advocate that grace, and grace alone, was God's method of salvation through Jesus. No works of man were required, or even beneficial or supportive, in the salvation of a person's soul. To Paul, God's love motivated Him to send Jesus, Jesus' death on the cross was the only requirement for atonement of sins, and believing on Jesus was the only thing necessary to receive God's forgiveness and gain eternal life.

Paul was *not* saying that the believers who returned to the Law were no longer covered by God's grace and forgiveness. Rather, he was saying that they had fallen away from God's provision of grace and bound themselves again to the constrictions of the Law. God had not cast them away; they had again taken upon themselves the yoke of the Law and had moved away from a position of grace.

To What Do You Fall?

The question certainly arises, "If you can fall from the provision of grace—God's unmerited love and favor as manifested by the death of Jesus Christ for sinners—to what is it that you fall?" The answer can only be, "To works." If you no longer choose to accept the fact that simple belief in Jesus Christ, receiving Him as Savior, is sufficient for everlasting life and a restored relationship with God . . . on what are you going to rely for your salvation? You will have to rely upon your good works. Paul says very clearly, "We through the Spirit eagerly wait for the hope of righteousness by faith" (Gal. 5:5). The Law won't provide what you are trusting it to provide, he says. Paul chooses instead to opt for *faith* as the means by which the Spirit puts a person into right standing with God (which is righteousness).

Paul goes on from these few verses to remind the brethren in Galatia that they have been called to *liberty*—not so they can sin, but so they might love and serve one another. He challenges them to walk in the Spirit so they won't fulfill the lusts of the flesh. He spells out clearly the lusts of the flesh and also the fruit of the Spirit. (See Gal. 5:19–25.)

One of Two Paths

In summary, Paul sets before the believers two paths they might take:

1. A path of the Law, which is filled with "don't do this, don't do that" commandments—a Law that points out man's sins and which is rooted in a concern with what *not* to do.
2. A path of grace, which is filled with "do this, do that" out of love for Christ—a path that points out the provision of the Holy Spirit to help us in right living and that is rooted in a freedom to do those things that are both pleasing to God and beneficial for life.

You cannot walk both paths simultaneously, Paul warns. If you walk the path of the Law, you will be turning your back on the path of grace. If you walk the path of grace, you will fulfill the Law but not be bound by it.

At no time does Paul indicate that these Galatians will lose their salvation. What they are in danger of losing are the joy of their salvation and the freedom of following the daily leading of the Holy Spirit!

- *Reread Galatians 5:1–6. What new insights do you have into this passage? (I encourage you to read the whole of Galatians— the letter only has six chapters. See this passage in the full context of Paul's discussion about slavery to the Law and the freedom associated with grace.)*

_____

_____

"Blotted" from the Book of Life

In the Revelation of Jesus Christ that was given to John, we find this passage that is often used to support a belief in the ability of a believer to fall from grace:

And to the angel of the church in Sardis write, "These things says He who has the seven Spirits of God and the seven stars: 'I know your works, that you have a name that you are alive, but you are dead. Be watchful, and strengthen the things which remain, that are ready to die, for I have not found your works perfect before God. Remember therefore how you have received and heard; hold fast and repent. Therefore if you will not watch, I will come upon you as a thief, and you will not know what hour I will come upon you. You have a few names even in Sardis who have not defiled their garments; and they shall walk with Me in white, for they are worthy. He who overcomes shall be clothed in white garments, and I will not blot out his name from the Book of Life; but I will confess his name before My Father and before His angels'" (Rev. 3:1–5).

The message of the Lord to the church in Sardis is directed toward a spiritual "deadness" that the Lord sees in those who claim to "have a name that you are alive, but you are dead." These are people who go through the motions of aligning themselves with the church and pursuing Christian disciplines, but their hearts are not truly following the leading of the Holy Spirit. Among them were those who were never genuinely born again, but who simply associated with the church and sought to have a godly reputation.

Certainly a number of people today are like the Sardinians. They attend church, they go through the motions that are acceptable, but they have not truly been born again. Outwardly, they appear to be right with God, but inwardly, they have never been truly born again.

Others in Sardis were believers who had truly accepted Christ, but then had become more concerned with outward behavior than inner spiritual growth. The Lord calls them to remember the time when they received and heard the gospel and to hold fast to the living faith within their hearts and to continue to sorrow for their sinful ways. These are people who think they have "done enough" to get into heaven, but now they are relying on their outward appearances and reputations more than they are pursuing the inner qualities and character that God desires for them.

Sardis was located at the junction of several major Roman roads and the citizens of Sardis were known not only for their luxurious, indulgent lifestyles, but also for their strong and zealous promotion of "emperor worship." The true believers in Sardis were very likely being called to repentance for slipping back into old patterns of behavior and making compromises with old beliefs.

The Great White Throne Judgment

The reference made in this warning to the believers at Sardis pertains to the "Book of Life." The judgment that involves the Book of Life is not a judgment of the lost, but a judgment of believers. It is also called the Great White Throne Judgment. We read about it in Revelation 20:11–15:

> Then I saw a great white throne and Him who sat on it, from whose face the earth and the heaven fled away. And there was found no place for them. And I saw the dead, small and great, standing before God, and books were opened. And another book was opened, which is the Book of Life. And the dead were judged according to their works, by the things which were written in the books. The sea gave up the dead who were in it, and Death and Hades delivered up the dead who were in them. And they were judged, each one according to his works. Then Death and Hades were cast into the lake of fire. This is the second death. And anyone not found written in the Book of Life was cast into the lake of fire.

The deeds in the Book of Life relate to the *rewards* that believers will be given. Those not in the book have already been judged by the time this Great White Throne Judgment takes place. Those not written in the book will be the ones who follow the "beast" that makes war against the saints. (See Rev. 13:7–8 and 17:8.) Their defeat is described in Revelation 19. At the time of the Great White Throne Judgment those *not* in the Book of Life will receive the punishment that comes as a result of their judgment: they are cast into the lake of fire. Those whose names *are* in the Book of Life will be granted their rewards according to their works as believers.

What is at stake for the believers in Sardis are their *rewards*—not the fact that they are saved. This matter of reward is also addressed in Revelation 22:19, where we have a warning that if anyone attempts to add or take away anything from the book of Revelation, God will "take away his part from the Book of Life."

Eternal *rewards* can be won and lost. The salvation of the true believer is not what is at stake here.

The main admonition to us today is this: Be *genuinely born again*. Don't accept any substitution for a true salvation—don't think that church attendance, church membership, participation in certain church activities, or any other outward involvement in Christian disciplines will save you. Only genuine belief in Jesus Christ as God's Son, sent to the cross to die for your sins, will result in your being born again. Only receiving Jesus Christ as your Savior will ensure that your name is written in the Book of Life.

- *What new insights do you have into these passages from the book of Revelation?*

_____

_____

Other Solemn Warnings

Various other passages in the Bible—such as Psalm 69, Matthew 24, John 15, Colossians 1, and 1 John 2—are sometimes used to support the belief that it is possible for born-again believers to fall from grace. When reading passages such as these, I encourage you to ask yourselves these questions:

- *Is the writer referring to a physical death or a spiritual death?* In some of the passages used to support falling from grace, a *physical* death is being described, not a spiritual death. For example, Psalm 69 refers to physical death, not spiritual death.
- *What time or era is being described by the author?* In Matthew 24–25, for example, Jesus is speaking of a time of Great Tribulation. Great deceit will fill the earth and the warning is to be watchful always for the Lord's coming, for the "elect" will be gathered to the Lord. Much of this teaching is *not* for believers.

• *Is the passage related to the way believers are to live their lives on this earth, or is it related to the salvation of the soul?* Often, you will need to see the broader context in which a selected group of verses appears. In Colossians 1:21–23, for example, we read:

> And you, who once were alienated and enemies in your mind by wicked works, yet now He has reconciled in the body of His flesh through death, to present you holy, and blameless, and above reproach in His sight—if indeed you continue in the faith, grounded and steadfast, and are not moved away from the hope of the gospel which you heard.

If one only reads these three verses, it may appear that a person is only going to be saved if he remains in faith and doesn't move away from the "hope of the gospel." The broader context of Colossians is this: Jesus Christ! Throughout this book, Paul lifts up Jesus as the Savior, the giver of wisdom, the principal agent of creation, and so forth. What is at stake for the Colossians is that they *continue* to place their trust in Jesus Christ and to live, pray, and speak (see Col. 4:1–6) in such a way that Jesus will have no qualms about the way they are living. Rather, He will find them to be living holy, blameless, and above-reproach lives. Paul warns the Colossians against the inadequacy of certain rituals and points them repeatedly toward the all-sufficiency of Christ and the new life He purchased for them. At no time is salvation at issue—but rather, the quality of life the believers are to have and the acclaim they are to win from the Lord by following Him with faith.

• *Is the passage about believers or nonbelievers?* John writes that some are "not of us" (1 John 2:19). That's certainly true today! Believers and nonbelievers live by different standards, have different perspectives, and are subject to different judgments. In 1 John 2, John gives a very clear delineation between believers and nonbelievers. At no time is he describing believers who have *become* nonbelievers—rather, he is describing nonbelievers as those who have never become believers. Those who are operating out of a sin nature simply cannot love or obey God's commandments as believers can.

This same difference is described by John in other terms in John 15. Those who do not abide in the true vine of Jesus Christ are "cast out as a branch" and they are subject to being thrown into the "fire" (v. 6). This refers to those who have never believed in Jesus and, therefore, have never truly abided in Him. Believers, in comparison, are pruned so that they will bear fruit.

- *Has the Lord ever given you a spiritual insight so that you were brought to a new level of understanding about a particular passage of Scripture? Did your new insight have anything to do with seeing the broader context or the correct context of the passage?*

  _____

  _____

- *In what ways is the Lord challenging you today regarding the eternal security of your salvation?*

  _____

  _____

LESSON 7

SOLEMN WARNINGS: PART 2

In the last lesson we covered several of the Scripture passages that are used to support the belief that it is possible for a born-again believer to lose his salvation or fall from grace. In this lesson, we will deal specifically with the verses in Hebrews that are often quoted by those who hold this position.

In several places within Hebrews, the author of this book warns readers of the perils of abandoning the Christian faith. As we did in the previous lesson, we must take a look at the audience to whom these warnings were made in order to have greater insight into the meaning of these passages.

In all probability the writer of Hebrews was addressing Jewish Christians. The book has several major themes that support this—repeated insistence that the old covenant was obsolete, arguments made with references to Old Testament Scriptures (which would have been known only by Jewish believers), and a concern that those reading the book not return to Judaism.

These believers had never seen nor heard Jesus personally (see Heb. 2:3), but they had faced intense opposition for believing in Him, including prison, insults, and confiscation of their property. (See Heb. 10:32–34.) Through it all, however, they had remained faithful to their newfound faith. But then some began to become disillusioned and to drift away (Heb. 2:1). Their tendency was to retreat back to Judaism, which was a religion that Rome allowed.

The author of Hebrews is intent on encouraging his Jewish Christian brothers and sisters to *keep* their faith in Jesus Christ. He points out Christ's superiority over the Old Testament prophets, angels, and even Moses. He argues superiority of Christ's priesthood to that of both Melchizedek and Aaron. He demonstrates the preeminence of the new covenant over the old. And the book ends with an encouragement to remain faithful in the light of those who have gone before them (likely those who had been persecuted and perhaps even killed for their faith in Christ). The passages that are used to argue a falling-from-grace position are interspersed within this overall argument being made to the Jewish believers.

It is important for us to recognize that these warnings are *not* being given to a group of people who are trying to make up their minds about Christ Jesus for the first time. The warnings are made to those who had expressed faith in Christ and were sincere enough in their belief in Christ to suffer.

Furthermore, we must recognize that the question with which this group was struggling was *not* whether they should abandon God and live a sinful life. They were not grappling with whether they should readopt a sin nature, or whether this was even possible. Rather, they were grappling with what "form of religion" they were going to follow.

These Jewish Christians are unusual in a peculiar way—they were attempting to decide if they would leave Christianity as a religion in order to adhere to a religion that demanded even more from them and allowed them less freedom! Rarely is that the case in our world. Most people opt for an easier way to please God, not a more difficult way.

What Hebrews Teaches Regarding Salvation

Before taking a look at the three most quoted passages of Hebrews regarding eternal security, let's consider for a moment what the book of Hebrews as a whole teaches about salvation. While we cannot do an entire survey of Hebrews in this one lesson, we can note these things about the book:

- No book in the New Testament other than the Gospel of John argues so conclusively in favor of a salvation that is eternally secure. The author clearly states that blood sacrifices of animals cannot accomplish what the death of Christ accomplished "once for all" (Heb. 9:26–27; 10:9–14).
- The author clearly states that Christians are sanctified or made holy through the death of Christ *for all time.* (See Heb. 10:5–14.)
- The author encourages the readers to "hold fast the confession of our hope without wavering" (Heb. 10:23). Many people who believe they can fall from grace question whether the blood of Jesus was fully adequate for their salvation. What they believe is that they have to "do their part" to ensure salvation—which is adding "works" to their faith. Those who believe they have to do something to ensure salvation will always waver in their hope because, intuitively and instinctively, they know their own fallibility and unreliability as human beings.

Overall the writer of Hebrews presents a very strong message for the complete adequacy of Christ's death as the sole means for our salvation, and encourages believers in Christ to "hold fast" to what they have done: they believed in and received Jesus as Savior.

What the Word Says	What the Word Says to Me
He then would have had to suffer often since the foundation of the world; but now, once at the end of the ages, He has appeared to put away sin by the sacrifice of Himself. And as it is appointed for	

men to die once, but after this the judgment, so Christ was offered once to bear the sins of many (Heb. 9:26–28).

When He came into the world, He said: "Sacrifice and offering You did not desire, But a body You have prepared for Me. In burnt offerings and sacrifices for sin You had no pleasure. Then I said, 'Behold, I have come . . . To do Your will, O God.'" . . . He takes away the first that He may establish the second. By that will we have been sanctified through the offering of the body of Jesus Christ once for all. . . . For by one offering He has perfected forever those who are being sanctified (Heb. 10:5–7, 9–10, 14).

Let us draw near with a true heart in full assurance of faith, having our hearts sprinkled from an evil conscience and our bodies washed with pure water. Let us hold fast the confession of our hope without wavering, for He who promised is faithful (Heb. 10:22–23).

It is highly unreasonable, in my opinion, to believe that an author who stands so strongly in favor of eternal security could also be an advocate for falling from grace. The overriding message of Hebrews is that Christ is our sufficiency; in His death is our eternal life. To add works to that provision of Christ is to misread, in my opinion, the true message of the author.

Warning #1: Do Not Drift or Neglect

Let us turn now to the three foremost words of warning that are offered in Hebrews. The first passage is Hebrews 2:1–3:

> Therefore we must give the more earnest heed to the things we have heard, lest we drift away. For if the word spoken through angels proved steadfast, and every transgression and disobedience received a just reward, how shall we escape if we neglect so great a salvation, which at the first began to be spoken by the Lord, and was confirmed to us by those who heard Him.

The author of Hebrews seems to take the tone of a teacher who catches a student nodding off during class. "Take earnest heed! Don't drift off!" That's the intent of the phrase, "lest we drift away." The term *drifting* implies a slow, gradual process. The author of Hebrews recognized that those he was addressing had the potential for losing interest in the things pertaining to salvation. They weren't drifting from a position of being saved—they were drifting in their ideas about religion. Just as no person comes to Christ by "drifting into" salvation, so no person can fall from grace by "drifting away" from Christ.

The author reminds them that a great deal is at stake if they "neglect" their salvation. Some people today seem to think that after they are saved, they don't need to attend church, read their Bibles, or pray—they say to themselves and others, "Well, I'm saved. That's all that matters." Not true! "Just being saved" is only the beginning of the Christian life. There is much growing to do and many rewards to attain. If a person "neglects" his salvation and fails to move forward in his faith, he will lose a great deal, even though he does not lose his salvation.

The overall intent of the author of Hebrews in this passage is to say, "Pay attention! This is important!" It is *not* a condemnation of those who have been saved and are now in danger of being lost.

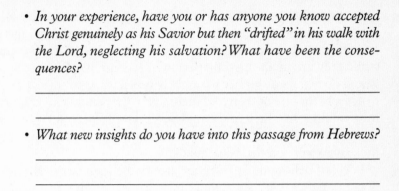

- *In your experience, have you or has anyone you know accepted Christ genuinely as his Savior but then "drifted" in his walk with the Lord, neglecting his salvation? What have been the consequences?*

_____

_____

- *What new insights do you have into this passage from Hebrews?*

_____

_____

Warning #2: No Falling Away

A second passage in Hebrews that is often cited as an argument for falling from grace is Hebrews 6:4–6:

> For it is impossible for those who were once enlightened, and have tasted the heavenly gift, and have become partakers of the Holy Spirit, and have tasted the good word of God and the powers of the age to come, if they fall away, to renew them again to repentance, since they crucify again for themselves the Son of God, and put Him to an open shame.

There are some who dismiss this passage as relating only to non-believers, or to those who have not been genuinely born again. I believe, however, that the author makes it very clear that they were enlightened, that they tasted the heavenly gift, that they were partakers of the heavenly gift (forgiveness and receiving the Holy Spirit), and that they tasted the good word of God (which means that they knew its promises to be true).

What does it mean for these genuine believers to fall away? That is the heart of the matter.

To say that they have fallen away from their position of saved believers in Christ and have thus *lost* their salvation would be a dire situation, indeed, for this passage says that a person who falls away can never regain what he has lost through future repentance. Most people who believe in falling from grace do not hold such a position—rather, they believe it is possible to repent and fall and repent and fall, with the hope that they will die or that the Lord will come while they are in an upswing period of repentance. We certainly would do a great disservice to nonbelievers if we encouraged them to accept Christ, but then told them that if they sinned in any way, they would lose Christ and could never have Him as their Savior in the future. We'd be far wiser to wait and win to the Lord only those who were on their deathbeds!

I do not believe this passage relates in the least to one's salvation, but rather that these people are being warned not to fall away from their active pursuit of the Christian faith . . . in other words, not to fall away into their old patterns of legalism and Jewish traditions. It is a warning against apostasy, which is the extreme falling away from the pursuit of Christ to completely ignore Christ and pursue another path.

No Return?

Why would it be impossible for such a person to return to Christ through repentance? Because such a person who had chosen another path would not even think to repent! Note very closely that the author does not say they cannot be forgiven, but that they will not be "renewed" through repentance.

In Romans 12:2 we find Paul's admonition to believers that they are *not* "conformed to this world," but that they "be transformed by the renewing of your mind," that they might "prove what is that good and acceptable and perfect will of God." Renewal is the process of transformation from the old way that we thought, acted, and felt prior to our acceptance of Christ Jesus as our Savior, to a new way that is made possible by the Holy Spirit dwelling within us. Renewal is the result of repentance and walking into a new way of life as the Holy Spirit leads and strengthens.

Those who were on the verge of returning to Judaism were in danger of no longer being sensitive to the leading and guiding of the Holy Spirit. They were in danger of no longer desiring to be renewed, and should that become the case, they would no longer have any desire to repent and walk into the newness of life that Christ offered to them and the Holy Spirit made possible for them.

There are a number of Christians today who know the right thing to do (as expressed in the Bible and as the Holy Spirit convicts them), but who simply choose *not* to be renewed in a specific area of their lives. They do not desire to repent and be transformed. Instead, they have chosen to live in a different way, to walk a different path. The result is that they have "fallen away" from the full potential they could have in Christ Jesus. Repentance is so far removed from their thinking that it is like a foreign concept to them. This is the situation that the author of Hebrews warns against!

The author goes on to say further that those who fall away revert to a belief in which Jesus somehow *deserved* to die for *His* misdeeds (which was the Jewish position regarding Christ), rather than Jesus *choosing* to lay down His life for *our* sins, so that we might have everlasting life and a fully restored relationship with our heavenly Father. Those who believe that Jesus *deserved* death, indeed, crucify Him again and bring shame to Him. They certainly are not likely to look to Him to lead them into a renewal of their lives.

- *In your experience, have you ever encountered those who came to Christ but then chose another path that was foreign to Christ and therefore, although they "knew" what to do in order to grow spiritually into the fullness of Christ Jesus, they had no desire to do it? What was the result?*

_____

_____

- *Can you empathize with how it might feel to turn away from one's potential in Christ and to pursue another path?*

_____

_____

Warning #3: No More Offering

The third passage often quoted in support of a falling-from-grace belief is Hebrews 10:26–31:

For if we sin willfully after we have received the knowledge of the truth, there no longer remains a sacrifice for sins, but a certain fearful expectation of judgment, and fiery indignation which will devour the adversaries. Anyone who has rejected Moses' law dies without mercy on the testimony of two or three witnesses. Of how much worse punishment, do you suppose, will he be thought worthy who has trampled the Son of God underfoot, counted the blood of the covenant by which he was sanctified a common thing, and insulted the Spirit of grace? For we know Him who said, "Vengeance is Mine, I will repay," says the Lord. And again, "The LORD will judge His people." It is a fearful thing to fall into the hands of the living God.

Reading only at the surface level, this passage seems to indicate that those who sin "willfully" after they have been saved will no longer be able to escape God's "fiery indignation." First, we should note that at no time in the New Testament is a distinction made between various types, levels, or categories of sin, including those who sin willfully and those who sin unknowingly. Neither does the Bible ever state that Christ died only for some sins and not others, or specifically for those sins before a person believes versus those after. In fact, Hebrews 10:12–14 says He offered "one sacrifice for sins forever."

Note also that this passage begins with the word *for*, which means that it relates to the information immediately preceding it. The verses that lead up to this warning are words of encouragement to follow through with a commitment to Christ in light of all He has done for believers. "Let us draw near with a true heart in full assurance of faith," the author writes (Heb. 10:22). "Let us hold fast the confession of our hope without wavering" and "let us consider one another in order to stir up love and good works" (vv. 23, 24).

The logical thing to ask after such statements is, "What if we don't?" The author of Hebrews anticipates this question and answers it.

Remember that the audience for these words is Jewish. They have lived their entire lives awaiting the Messiah, One who would establish a new covenant so powerful that God would forget their sins forever. (See Heb. 10:17.)

The author reminds these Jewish believers that their next encounter is not going to be an encounter with Christ the Savior, but with Christ the Judge. Rather than being bad news that "there no longer remains a sacrifice for sin," this word is *good* news. The fact is, the sacrifice for sin has been made! The only bad news is that God is not fond of quitters.

Again, the author is attempting to prod these believers on to godly living. The "fire" of which the author speaks is not a fire of eternal punishment—the "lake of fire" that we associate with Revelation. Rather, it is the "fiery indignation" of God's judgment. Certainly, the author states, God will judge those who turn away from Christ as Messiah. They will be chastised sharply in this life, and in eternity they will not receive any of the rewards they could have had. If one compares all of the rewards that are *possible* for these believers to attain—as well as all of the greatness of Christlike character that might have been produced in them through the transforming work of the Holy Spirit—to what they will have if they return to a life of strict Judaism, their loss will be great indeed! They truly will suffer loss, and they should rightfully fear such a suffering, but at no time does the author state that their eternal salvation is in jeopardy. Rather, all of their rewards and their standing within the body of Christ are at stake.

Truly it is "terrifying" to think of all that a person *might* have been and *might* have become and *might* have been rewarded. To the author of Hebrews, the possibility that one might stand before the judgment seat of Christ and see all his works burned to ashes would be a "much worse punishment" than even death itself (Heb. 10:29). Regret is a terrible state in which to live. The author of Hebrews makes it very clear that if a person is born again and then returns to a life under the Law, such a person will have chosen just such a shadowy, foreboding, awful place to dwell spiritually.

• *What new insights do you have into this passage from Hebrews?*

_____

_____

• *How do you feel about the fact that a believer has no "excuse" for not moving forward in his or her faith after accepting Jesus Christ as Savior?*

_____

_____

Repeatedly, the author of Hebrews states that Christ made "one offering" for sin and that this was an eternal and never-to-be-repeated sacrifice. If we reject Christ's provision for our sin, we certainly are in dire danger of being lost forever. If we accept Christ's provision but do not continue to trust in Christ to bring us to the fullness of character that He desires for us, then we are in dire danger of losing the rewards we might otherwise have received. That is the message of Hebrews—a message that most certainly is a strong warning to those believers who might be wavering in their commitment to follow Christ's example or are hesitant in their willingness to follow the leading of the Holy Spirit. It is not, however, a warning that a person can lose the salvation that Christ has purchased with His blood and offered freely to those who believe.

• *In what ways are you being challenged regarding eternal security?*

_____

_____

LESSON 8

A LICENSE TO SIN?

Many people seem to believe that if one believes in the eternal security of salvation, that person then has a license to sin. Absolutely not!

At no time in Scripture do we find God winking at sin, diminishing the importance of sin, or allowing sin to go without serious consequences. There is never a license to sin, before or after one's spiritual rebirth.

"But," a person might say, "if a person can never lose his salvation, what keeps that person from living any way he desires or of sinning all he wants? He'll still make it to heaven, so what difference does future sin make?"

In the first place, a person who is genuinely born again will not *want* to sin or live "any way he desires." If a person still has a strong desire to sin and to live in a manner that is contrary to the will of God, he very likely has not been genuinely born again. When a person has experienced a spiritual new birth, he is a new creature and will not *want* to sin.

Second, "just making heaven" is a poor excuse for an eternal state of being. At stake is a great loss of eternal reward, which we will cover in the next lesson.

Third, the person who pursues sin after being born again is a person who is going to experience God's chastening on this earth. Although not all pain and suffering are related to chastening, certainly chastening can include pain, suffering, loss, and trouble. A person who accepts Christ and then refuses all prompting of the Holy Spirit to repent and be transformed in character and behavior is a person who is likely going to experience a certain amount of "hell on earth," even though he or she may escape the eternal fires of hell.

In this lesson, we will take a look at both mankind's sin nature and the believer's sinful deeds, and the consequences associated with each. First, however, we'll take a brief look at the Holy Spirit's relationship to us before and after our salvation.

The Holy Spirit's Roles Related to Our Sin

Prior to our conversion, the Holy Spirit is at work in our lives to *bring* us to a recognition of our sin nature and to prompt us to accept Jesus as our Savior. The Holy Spirit *woos* us to Christ. The conviction that we experience prior to our spiritual rebirth is a conviction that is not only related to our sinful deeds, but to the greater truth that we *are* sinners—we have a sin nature that must be changed. The Holy Spirit is relentless in His pursuit of us, although the unsaved person may not be aware of the Holy Spirit's work or may even deny His existence.

The person who has not been born again is subject to eternal death. That is the punishment awaiting any person who has not received Christ Jesus as Savior. This punishment is related to the sin *nature* of an unsaved person, not to specific sin *deeds*.

The conviction of the Holy Spirit in the unbeliever's life is related to the Word of God—when an unbeliever hears the Word of God, there is a convicting power to it that causes a person to have to confront his lack of relationship with God. The unsaved person has a haunting "knowing" that he is estranged from God, now and forever, unless the very "state" of his soul is changed. The person has the knowledge that he is sinful, needs forgiveness, and at the same time, the knowledge that he cannot forgive himself or alter his own nature (regardless of how he might seek to amend his behavior).

• *Recall how you felt and what you "knew" to be true about your-self and your sin prior to being born again.*

What the Word Says

For the wages of sin is death, but the gift of God is eternal life in Christ Jesus our Lord (Rom. 6:23).

Anyone not found written in the Book of Life was cast into the lake of fire (Rev. 20:15).

The sting of death is sin (1 Cor. 15:56).

[Jesus said of the Holy Spirit:] And when He has come, He will convict the world of sin, and of righteousness, and of judgment (John 16:8).

How then shall they call on Him in whom they have not believed? And how shall they believe in Him of whom they have not heard? And how shall they hear without a preacher? . . . So then faith comes by hearing, and hearing by the word of God (Rom. 10:14, 17).

He who has the Son has life; he who does not have the Son of God does not have life (1 John 5:12).

What the Word Says to Me

The Holy Spirit's work in our lives after we are born again is very different. The Holy Spirit *indwells* the one who receives Christ Jesus as Savior. No longer is He at work externally, but now internally. The Holy Spirit illuminates the Word of God as we read it or brings to our remembrance the Word of God to prick our conscience and lead us to make right decisions and walk in right paths. The Holy Spirit functions within us as the Spirit of Truth, showing us God's perfect will.

When we fail to listen to the Holy Spirit with our spiritual ears, and we choose to walk in our own ways rather than in God's way, the Holy Spirit chastises us. We feel uncomfortable, frustrated, and uneasy in our spirits. We have a knowing that we are disobeying God's plan for our lives and that we are not becoming the people God desires for us to be. The nudge of the Holy Spirit is toward our *repentance*—of our recognizing our sinful attitudes and deeds, of asking God to forgive us, and of asking the Holy Spirit to help us to have the courage to withstand temptation and follow explicitly the path God has set before us.

The Holy Spirit both leads us and enables us to act. When we fail to receive His guidance and His help, we grieve Him. We fall into error; we fail to live the way God desires for us to live. He is grieved on our behalf (see Eph. 4:30), and He seeks to bring us back into alignment with God's plan for us. His efforts to *correct* us and teach us are what we perceive as God's chastisement.

What the Word Says

[Jesus said:] When the Helper comes, whom I shall send to you from the Father, the Spirit of truth who proceeds from the Father, He will testify of Me. . . . [The Holy Spirit] will guide you into all truth; for He will not speak on His own authority, but whatever He hears He will speak; and He will tell you things to come. He will glorify Me, for He will take of what is Mine and declare it to you (John 15:26; 16:13–14).

What the Word Says to Me

_____
_____
_____
_____
_____
_____
_____
_____
_____
_____
_____
_____
_____

And do not grieve the Holy Spirit
of God, by whom you were sealed
for the day of redemption. Let all
bitterness, wrath, anger, clamor,
and evil speaking be put away
from you, with all malice. And be
kind to one another, tender-
hearted, forgiving one another,
even as God in Christ forgave you
(Eph. 4:30–32).

Chastening vs. Punishment

The nonbeliever is subject to punishment. Punishment is irreversible; it is the consequence for an unchanged spiritual *state of
being*. Punishment is, in effect, the aftermath of a "final sentenc-
ing."

The believer is subject to chastening, not punishment. Chastening is for the purpose of teaching, training, and correcting. It is
always exercised for the *good* of the person—in other words, so that
the person might change his ways and become more like Jesus
Christ in character, attitude, and behavior. Chastening occurs in
the wake of specific *sinful deeds*. It occurs because our heavenly
Father loves us enough to want to spare us the consequences of
sin. He wants us to grow into the likeness of Jesus Christ—He wants
us to become all we can possibly be! (See Heb. 12:6.)

Although chastening is certainly for our good, it is nonetheless
painful. Those who are born again and then choose to sin will
not find that their sin goes unchastened—rather, they will discover
that the longer they continue to engage in sinful attitudes and deeds,
the *stronger* the chastening will become. The best thing to do when
you are being chastened by God is to "yield" immediately, acknowledging your sin, seeking forgiveness, and asking God to help you
to change your attitude or your behavior. You can greatly lessen the
pain of chastening if you will respond quickly and *learn* from it.
Not only will the pain be eliminated, but in learning from your
chastening, you will actually be "trained" into the right way to live
and experience God's peace. (See Heb. 12:11.)

• *In your life, have you experienced chastisement? How did you feel? What was the result?*

_____

_____

What the Word Says

We are chastened by the Lord, that we may not be condemned with the world (1 Cor. 11:32).

You should know in your heart that as a man chastens his son, so the LORD your God chastens you. Therefore, you shall keep the commandments of the LORD your God, to walk in His ways and to fear Him. For the LORD your God is bringing you into a good land (Deut. 8:5–7).

My son, do not despise the chastening of the LORD,
Nor be discouraged when you are rebuked by Him;
For whom the LORD loves He chastens,
And scourges every son whom He receives.
If you endure chastening, God deals with you as with sons; for what son is there whom a father does not chasten? . . . Furthermore, we have had human fathers who corrected us, and we
paid them respect. Shall we not much more readily be in subjec-
tion to the Father of spirits and live? For they indeed for a few days chastened us as seemed best

What the Word Says to Me

----

to them, but He for our profit,   ------------------------------
that we may be partakers of His   ------------------------------
holiness. Now no chastening   ------------------------------
seems to be joyful for the present,   ------------------------------
but painful; nevertheless, after-   ------------------------------
ward it yields the peaceable fruit   ------------------------------
of righteousness to those who   ------------------------------
have been trained by it (Heb.   ------------------------------
12:5–7, 9–11; see also Prov.   ------------------------------
3:11–12).   ------------------------------

• *In what ways are you feeling challenged in your spirit today?*

_____

_____

Eliminating the Desire to Sin

The Holy Spirit also works within the believer to generate a *hunger and thirst* for righteousness, which might also be stated as *a lack of desire to sin*. The Holy Spirit gives us a "want to" regarding obedience to the commandments of God (in place of a "have to" spirit, which is generally how the unbeliever regards God's laws).

Knowing that we are saved forever does not create in the genuine believer a freedom to sin, but rather, a freedom from all desire to sin! The true believer is not only out of the bondage of sin, but the true believer will not have any desire to reenter that bondage.

John wrote, "We know that whoever is born of God does not sin; but he who has been born of God keeps himself" (1 John 5:18). John was not saying that the born-again believer will never again sin or err; rather, this verse is the conclusion to the several verses that go before it—verses that are about the "sin which leads to death." John is saying that the person who is born again no longer sins the sin that leads to death. Rather, the born-again believer has a new identity and a new desire to be so sensitive and obedient to the leading of the Holy Spirit that he will not sin. The genuine born-again believer will choose, by an act of the will, to "[keep] himself" away from sin and temptation. He will choose, by an act of the will, to walk in paths of righteousness.

- *How did you feel when you knew that you were born again and that you had been fully forgiven from your sin nature? How do that "freedom and peace" relate to your desire not to sin now?*

  _____

  _____

- *Have you had experiences in which you knew the Holy Spirit was leading you into right attitudes and behaviors, as well as helping you to adopt those attitudes and engage in those behaviors?*

  _____

  _____

What the Word Says

If we say that we have fellowship with Him, and walk in darkness, we lie and do not practice the truth. But if we walk in the light as He is in the light, we have fellowship with one another, and the blood of Jesus Christ His Son cleanses us from all sin (1 John 1:6–7).

Whoever keeps His word, truly the love of God is perfected in him. By this we know that we are in Him. He who says he abides in Him ought himself also to walk just as He walked (1 John 2:5–6).

We know that whoever is born of God does not sin; but he who has been born of God keeps himself, and the wicked one does not touch him (1 John 5:18).

What the Word Says to Me

_____

_____

_____

_____

_____

_____

_____

_____

_____

_____

_____

_____

_____

_____

_____

_____

_____

_____

What About the Unpardonable Sin?

Through the years I have talked with a number of Christians who were afraid they might have committed "the unpardonable sin." There are hundreds of verses in the Bible that promise forgiveness of sins, but only one passage refers to an unforgivable sin. We find it in Matthew 12:31–32, where Jesus said:

> Therefore I say to you, every sin and blasphemy will be forgiven men, but the blasphemy against the Spirit will not be forgiven men. Anyone who speaks a word against the Son of Man, it will be forgiven him; but whoever speaks against the Holy Spirit, it will not be forgiven him, either in this age or in the age to come.

Let's understand the context of this verse. Jesus had healed a demon-possessed man who was blind and dumb. The multitudes began to question, "Could this be the Son of David?" The Pharisees responded to the multitudes by declaring that Jesus cast out demons by the power of Beelzebub—in other words, that Jesus was controlled by the chief of all demons. They were engaging in *blasphemy*, which is defined as "defiant irreverence."

The Pharisees had seen proof after proof that Jesus was who He claimed to be. They couldn't escape the fact that what He was doing was supernatural in nature. But instead of acknowledging what I believe they knew in their hearts to be true, they attributed the supernatural power of Jesus to Satan, rather than to the Holy Spirit. Jesus' rebuke was *directly and solely* for these false teachers in this particular setting. Jesus was saying, in effect, "If these Pharisees cannot see the truth that I do what I do by the power of the Holy Spirit, they will never come to believe in Me and they will be lost forever. If they have so hardened their hearts against the Holy Spirit that they cannot recognize Him at work, they will not be able to believe in Me, now or in the future."

Christ is not in the world now as He was then. Although the Holy Spirit is still accomplishing supernatural things through His servants, those servants are merely representatives of the King. The circumstances of Matthew 12 make it impossible for this sin to take place today. The Bible clearly states, "Whoever calls on the name of the LORD shall be saved" (Rom. 10:13.) There is no invitation to salvation or promise related to God's forgiveness that has an "exception clause" that reads, "unless you commit the unpardonable sin."

Although there is no unpardonable sin today, there is an unpardonable *state of unbelief*. There is no pardon for a person who dies in unbelief. The good news, however, is that a person does not need to remain in this state of unbelief. He or she can choose to believe in Jesus and receive Him as their Savior!

- *What new insights do you have into Matthew 12:31–32?*

  _____

  _____

Walking in Freedom

The promise of the Holy Spirit to every believer is this: "Listen to Me and obey My voice, and I will keep you free from sin's bondage." The Holy Spirit does not lead us into sin or into the temptation to sin. Rather, He delivers us from all evil. You can choose to walk in the freedom *from sin*—and what a great freedom that is. Never do we have a freedom *to* sin, but we do have a great promise of freedom to live *apart* from sin!

What the Word Says

Let no one say when he is tempted, "I am tempted by God"; for God cannot be tempted by evil, nor does He Himself tempt anyone. But each one is tempted when he is drawn away by his own desires and enticed (James 1:13–14).

Do not love the world or the things in the world. If anyone

What the Word Says to Me

_____

_____

_____

_____

_____

_____

_____

_____

_____

_____

loves the world, the love of the
Father is not in him. For all that is
in the world—the lust of the flesh,
the lust of the eyes, and the pride
of life—is not of the Father but is
of the world. And the world is
passing away, and the lust of it;
but he who does the will of God
abides forever (1 John 2:15–17).

• *How do you feel about the possibility that you do not NEED to sin, but can trust the Holy Spirit to keep you from sin and temptation?*

• *In what ways are you feeling challenged in your spirit today?*

• *What new insights do you have into the eternal security of your salvation, and especially as the security of your salvation relates to sin?*

ETERNAL REWARDS

Eternal security is not equal to eternal rewards. Rewards are related to our *works* as believers—not only what we do for the Lord, but the works that we allow the Lord to do in us.

"Works," from a Bible perspective, include:

- Attitudes
- Motives
- Conduct
- Service

On these two points we must be very clear:

1. *Works can never earn salvation. We are saved solely by our faith in the Lord Jesus Christ as God's Son and our Savior.*
2. *All of the works of the believer are evaluated by the Lord. Works are related to the rewards each believer will receive from the Lord. Some rewards may be received in this life, but the vast majority of our rewards are reserved for us to receive in eternity.*

Many Christians seem to think, *I just want to get into heaven. I'll be satisfied if I can just get through the pearly gates.* That is not at all the attitude that God desires for us to have. Our goal as Christians should be to live in a way that will *be highly rewarded* by the Lord. It should be the desire of every believer to hear the Lord say one day, "*Well done*, thou good and faithful servant."

All Works Are Evaluated

The Scriptures declare repeatedly that all of our works after salvation are evaluated. We each will be fully accountable for our lives and how we spent our time, talents, and resources. There is no such thing as "neutrality" when it comes to our attitudes, motives, deeds, and behaviors after we are saved. Every deed, and every lack of deed, is subject to judgment. As we read in Colossians 3:23–25, we will receive "payment" for all that we do:

> And whatever you do, do it heartily, as to the Lord and not to men, knowing that from the Lord you will receive the reward of the inheritance; for you serve the Lord Christ. But he who does wrong will be repaid for what he has done, and there is no partiality.

Rewards and Repayments

In the first few chapters of Revelation, we find a sharp demarcation between "rewards" for service to the Lord and "repayment" for wrongs. Here are just a few of these contrasts:

- "Nevertheless I have this against you, that you have left your first love. Remember therefore from where you have fallen; repent and do the first works, or else I will come to you quickly and remove your lampstand from its place—unless you repent. . . . To him who overcomes I will give to eat from the tree of life, which is in the midst of the Paradise of God" (Rev. 2:4–5, 7).
- "I have a few things against you, because you have there those who hold the doctrine of Balaam, who taught Balak to put a stumbling block before the children of Israel, to eat things sacrificed to idols, and to commit sexual immorality. . . . Repent, or else I will come to you quickly

and will fight against them with the sword of My mouth. . . . To him who overcomes I will give some of the hidden manna to eat. And I will give him a white stone, and on the stone a new name written which no one knows except him who receives it" (Rev. 2:14, 16–17).

- "I know your works, love, service, faith, and your patience; and as for your works, the last are more than the first. Nevertheless I have a few things against you, because you allow that woman Jezebel, who calls herself a prophetess, to teach and seduce My servants to commit sexual immorality and eat things sacrificed to idols. And I gave her time to repent of her sexual immorality, and she did not repent. Indeed I will cast her into a sickbed, and those who commit adultery with her into great tribulation, unless they repent of their deeds. I will kill her children with death, and all the churches shall know that I am He who searches the minds and hearts. And I will give to each one of you according to your works. . . . He who overcomes, and keeps My works until the end, to him I will give power over the nations" (Rev. 2:19–23, 26).

Surely there can be no doubt that God's "rewards" are generous and life-giving and His "repayments" are to be avoided!

- *What new insights do you have into these passages of Scripture and eternal rewards?*

_____

_____

What the Word Says	What the Word Says to Me
He is a rewarder of those who diligently seek Him (Heb. 11:6).	_____ _____
Do not be deceived, God is not mocked; for whatever a man sows, that he will also reap. For he who sows to his flesh will of the flesh	_____ _____ _____ _____

reap corruption, but he who sows to the Spirit will of the Spirit reap everlasting life. And let us not grow weary while doing good, for in due season we shall reap if we do not lose heart. Therefore, as we have opportunity, let us do good to all, especially to those who are of the household of faith (Gal. 6:7–10).

He who judges me is the Lord. Therefore judge nothing before the time, until the Lord comes, who will both bring to light the hidden things of darkness and reveal the counsels of the hearts. Then each one's praise will come from God (1 Cor. 4:4–5).

Therefore we make it our aim . . . to be well pleasing to Him. For we must all appear before the judgment seat of Christ, that each one may receive the things done in the body, according to what he has done, whether good or bad. Knowing, therefore, the terror of the Lord, we persuade men (2 Cor. 5:9–11).

• *In what ways are you feeling challenged in your spirit today?*

No Tolerance for the "Lukewarm"

The Lord clearly desires for His people to desire what He desires, which is our highest, most joyful, fulfilling, and eternal good. We read in Revelation 3:15–16 these sobering words:

I know your works, that you are neither cold nor hot. I could wish you were cold or hot. So then, because you are lukewarm, and neither cold nor hot, I will vomit you out of My mouth.

Furthermore, the Lord desires these things of us:

- That we seek what the *Lord* defines as spiritual riches and genuine spiritual wealth—and that we continue to pursue all that the Lord has for us, never satisfied with our current level of spiritual maturity. No part of us is yet fully like Jesus Christ. There is always more of His character that we must aspire to attain. For example:

  - That we be more and more refined and made pure in spirit.
  - That we have greater and greater insight into God's Word and His plan and purpose for our lives.
  - That we be "zealous" for the things of the Lord.
  - That we long above all things to allow the Lord entrance into every area of our lives, every minute of our lives, and to develop an intimate relationship with Him. (See Rev. 3:17–20.)

We never "arrive" as Christians. Our desire must be to pursue *intensely* and with great *focus* of purpose the fullness of Christ Jesus.

What the Word Says	What the Word Says to Me
[The Lord said,] Because you say, "I am rich, have become wealthy, and have need of nothing"—and do not know that you are wretched, miserable, poor, blind, and naked—I counsel you to buy from Me gold refined in the fire, that you may be rich; and white garments, that you may be clothed, that the shame of your	

nakedness may not be revealed;
and anoint your eyes with eye
salve, that you may see. As many
as I love, I rebuke and chasten.
Therefore be zealous and repent.
Behold, I stand at the door and
knock. If anyone hears My voice
and opens the door, I will come in
to him and dine with him, and he
with Me (Rev. 3:17–20).

• *In what ways are you feeling challenged in your spirit?*

_____

_____

Choosing the Best Building Materials

The apostle Paul wrote to the Corinthians a very clear word picture regarding the works of believers:

> According to the grace of God which was given to me, as a wise master builder I have laid the foundation, and another builds on it. But let each one take heed how he builds on it. For no other foundation can anyone lay than that which is laid, which is Jesus Christ. Now if anyone builds on this foundation with gold, silver, precious stones, wood, hay, straw, each one's work will become clear; for the Day will declare it, because it will be revealed by fire; and the fire will test each one's work, of what sort it is. . . . If anyone's work is burned, he will suffer loss; but he himself will be saved, yet so as through fire (1 Cor. 3:10–15).

Consider two things about this passage. *First, Paul characterizes our works as being either combustible or incombustible.* When our works are evaluated in eternity, some of them are going to be reduced to a pile of ashes. We will have invested our time, talents, and resources into things that simply have no lasting value. Other works will be ones that remain and if anything, become purer and brighter when tested by fire. We each are called to set as our first priority the things of God—seeking His kingdom on a daily, even hourly basis is the most important priority we can have (see Matt. 6:10). If we make the Lord's will and the Lord's life *our* will and our life, all other things fall into place. When we put our thoughts, words, and deeds into the context of eternity, we generally have a clearer picture of what is truly important and what has "lasting" value. Only those things that are done by and for Christ Jesus will last forever.

- *In your life, can you identify thoughts, words, and deeds that might be regarded as wood, hay, and stubble? Gold, silver, and precious stones?*

_____

_____

Second, Paul speaks of building on a foundation with either wood, hay, and stubble, or with gold, silver, and precious stones. What is this foundation on which we are building? Paul states, "We are God's fellow workers; you are God's field, you are God's building" (1 Cor. 3:9). The building materials Paul describes are ones used to *build up other people*. Paul is describing the character of our witness—the lasting value of our service or ministry to others. Can anything be of more value to a sinner than a person sharing the gospel of Jesus Christ with him? Can anything be of more help to a hurting person than to experience a generous and tangible outpouring of God's love? Can anything be of greater value to the person who is depressed, oppressed, or in bondage than to be set free to experience the love and joy of Christ Jesus?

We must make it our number one intent to share all that we have of Christ with as many as possible in any given day of our lives. In this way, we "build" on the foundation of Christ Jesus that has been laid by the apostles and by generation after generation of faithful believers. In this way, we extend the gospel of Christ Jesus.

• *In your life, can you identify others who have built upon the foundation of Christ in your life, and in a way that is eternally valuable?*

_____

_____

What the Word Says	What the Word Says to Me
Your kingdom come. Your will be done On earth as it is in heaven (Matt. 6:10).	
Seek first the kingdom of God and His righteousness, and all these things shall be added to you (Matt. 6:33).	

• *Read Romans 12. Note in what ways the challenge to "present your bodies a living sacrifice, holy, acceptable to God" might be likened to building on a foundation of Christ with gold, silver, and precious stones.*

_____

_____

• *In what ways are you feeling challenged in your spirit?*

_____

_____

Not All Positions in Eternity Are Equal

The saints in heaven are not all going to have the same roles or occupy the same positions of authority. Some who are in great positions of power and authority here on earth, for example, will not have any power or authority in heaven. Others who seem to be the last or the least here on earth will be among those who have authority and power in heaven. God will evaluate the intent, faithfulness, and purity of each person's heart, and on that basis, establish the "rulership" of heaven. (See Matt. 19:30.)

We also read in the Scriptures about various "crowns" that will be given to believers. Crowns, of course, are signs of authority. While all of these crowns will be cast at the feet of Jesus—in deference to His ultimate authority over all things—these crowns are given to believers as part of their eternal reward. (See Rev. 4:4, 10).

Not the Same Degree of Joy

Furthermore, not all believers in heaven will be able to enjoy heaven to the same degree. We all take comfort from these words in Revelation 21:3–4:

> God Himself will be with them and be their God. And God will wipe away every tear from their eyes; there shall be no more death, nor sorrow, nor crying. There shall be no more pain, for the former things have passed away.

Life in heaven will bear these characteristics for *all* who occupy the eternal home God has for them. But the Scriptures also speak of a growing maturity of faith that will produce rewards. In 2 Corinthians 3:18 we read:

> But we all, with unveiled face, beholding as in a mirror the glory of the Lord, are being transformed into the same image from glory to glory, just as by the Spirit of the Lord.

Those who allow the Holy Spirit to transform their lives and bring about deep spiritual maturity are going to be able to take in, or experience, more of the glory of the Lord in eternity. They are going to have a greater capacity for joy, a greater capacity for praise, a deeper and richer understanding of God, and a closer intimacy with the Father.

What the Word Says	What the Word Says to Me
[Jesus taught His disciples:] Assuredly I say to you, that in the	

regeneration, when the Son of Man sits on the throne of His glory, you who have followed Me will also sit on twelve thrones, judging the twelve tribes of Israel. And everyone who has left houses or brothers or sisters or father or mother or wife or children or lands, for My name's sake, shall receive a hundredfold, and inherit eternal life. But many who are first will be last, and the last first (Matt. 19:28–30).

Around the throne were twenty-four thrones, and on the thrones I saw twenty-four elders sitting, clothed in white robes; and they had crowns of gold on their heads (Rev. 4:4).

On What Basis Are We Judged?

At no time in the Scriptures do we find that we are going to be compared to *others* when our works as believers are judged. Rather, what we do and are will be judged against our God-given potential and God's plan for our lives.

We each have been given very specific talents, opportunities, privileges, and a measure of time. What we *do* with God's gifts to us, and what we allow God to do in us and through us, are what will be judged.

As you read the passage of Scripture that follows, note especially these things:

- We are going to be judged on the basis of what we do to others.
- We are going to be judged on the degree to which we know and prepare ourselves to do the will of our Master.

- We are going to be judged according to how much has been given to us or entrusted to us.

We all are the servants of God. Some are aware that they are servants and others do not seem to be aware, yet we are all servants of God nonetheless. Those who do nothing with regard to Jesus Christ after hearing the gospel, assuming that there is no punishment for their sinful deeds but choosing instead to live unto themselves, which inevitably means mistreating others, will be those who are destroyed. They are the nonbelievers.

Others who have not ever heard the gospel (those who "do not know") will receive a much lesser punishment.

What the Word Says

And the Lord said, "Who then is that faithful and wise steward, whom his master will make ruler over his household, to give them their portion of food in due season? Blessed is that servant whom the master will find so doing when he comes. Truly, I say to you that he will make him ruler over all that he has. But if that servant says in his heart, 'My master is delaying his coming,' and begins to beat the male and female servants, and to eat and drink and be drunk, the master of that servant will come on a day when he is not looking for him, and at an hour when he is not aware, and will cut him in two and appoint him his portion with the unbelievers. And that servant who knew his master's will, and did not prepare himself or do according to his will, shall be beaten with many stripes.

What the Word Says to Me

But he who did not know, yet committed things deserving of stripes, shall be beaten with few. For everyone to whom much is given, from him much will be required; and to whom much has been committed, of him they will ask the more" (Luke 12:42–48).

- *Reflect upon your own life. What have you been given? What has been committed or entrusted to you? For what are you responsible before the Lord?*

  _____

  _____

- *In what ways are you being challenged in your understanding of eternal security and eternal rewards?*

  _____

  _____

LIVING IN THE ASSURANCE OF ETERNAL SECURITY

I have never met a Christian who has lost his salvation. However, I have met plenty who have lost their *assurance*. Our *security* rests in the hands of an unconditionally loving heavenly Father who gave His best, His only begotten Son, Jesus Christ, to ensure our fellowship with Him forever. Our *assurance* rests in understanding and accepting His provision and the truth that our salvation from sin's consequences is eternally secure.

There are three things that can rob us of our assurance. We must be on guard against them at all times:

1. Guilt, which arises when we do not seek forgiveness for our sins
2. Doubt that produces fear
3. Pride and feelings of self-sufficiency

Guilt Can Rob Us of Assurance

Guilt is the natural response to sin. Most people are trained from an early age to have an understanding between right and wrong. When we know we have done wrong, we *expect* a disciplinary response, and until we receive it, we live in anticipation of it. We know we deserve chastening or punishment. The anticipation of punishment and chastening is guilt.

The problem we have among born-again believers is that they have either ascribed the wrong "punishment" to their sins, or they have not sought and received the forgiveness that God makes available to them.

When we sin as believers, we must go immediately to our heavenly Father and ask His forgiveness. We must go with the assurance that when we ask, He forgives. We then must move forward in our lives, forgiving ourselves even as God has forgiven us. We are wise to seek to make amends to those we may have hurt by our sin, but we must not continue to harbor guilt for something God has forgiven.

Then, we must take the additional step of asking the Holy Spirit to help us *not* to engage in that sin again. We must choose to be sensitive to His leading us *away* from temptation. We must ask for His help to withstand temptation if temptation arises. (See Matt. 6:13.)

In my ministry, I have encountered a number of people who seem to think they have sinned too many times since their salvation for God to continue to extend His mercy and forgiveness to them. They say, in effect, "I've worn out God's patience. Surely He can't continue to forgive me since I've sinned so many times, or committed such a great sin." The fact is, God's mercy and forgiveness cannot be measured in human terms; God's capacity to forgive is as infinite as God.

No matter the nature or quantity of your sin, there is a "cure" for sin and guilt: God's forgiveness! Turn to the Lord with your guilt and receive His forgiveness. Do not let guilt rob you of your assurance that you are saved and eternally secure in your relationship with your loving heavenly Father.

What the Word Says

If we confess our sins, He is faithful and just to forgive us our sins and to cleanse us from all unrighteousness (1 John 1:9).

What the Word Says to Me

They refused to obey,
And they were not mindful of
Your wonders
That You did among them.
But they hardened their necks,
And in their rebellion they
appointed a leader
To return to their bondage.
But You are God,
Ready to pardon,
Gracious and merciful,
Slow to anger,
Abundant in kindness,
And did not forsake them. . . .
You also gave Your good Spirit to
instruct them (Neh. 9:17, 20).

The Lord is not slack concerning
His promise, as some count slack-
ness, but is longsuffering toward
us, not willing that any should
perish but that all should come to
repentance (2 Peter 3:9).

But You, O Lord, are a God full of
compassion, and gracious,
Longsuffering and abundant in
mercy and truth (Ps. 86:15).

[Jesus taught His disciples to
pray:] Do not lead us into temptation,
But deliver us from the evil one
(Matt. 6:13).

Doubt-Based Fear Can Rob
Us of Assurance

Fear of God's punishments can cause paralysis in a believer, even
to the point where the person no longer feels free to serve others

or to minister in ways that the Holy Spirit desires. Such a gripping fear is a work of Satan. It is rooted in Satan's lies about God, which cause the person to doubt God's love and mercy.

The basic lie that Satan feeds to a believer is this: "God is a hard taskmaster; He demands absolute perfection and obedience. He punishes severely all those who disobey Him." The devil will never tell a person how much God loves him, or how God has provided the means for a person to have his sin nature transformed through believing in Jesus Christ as his Savior.

What motivated God to send Jesus to die on the cross in your place? Love. Jesus said it plainly, "For God *so loved the world . . .*" (John 3:16 italics added). The sole motivation for God's mercy and kindness is love—a love of such magnitude that all human illustrations fall short, a love that is unconditional at its core with no hidden agendas and no fine print. God's love is such that He accepts us just the way we are, but He refuses to leave us there.

Our expression of faith in Jesus places us into an unconditional, loving relationship with our heavenly Father. His offer of salvation is made to all people everywhere. Some choose to accept it by faith, others will reject it. But the offer remains. Such is the nature of God's love.

The more a person meditates and reflects on the nature of God's unconditional love, the more absurd it sounds when someone begins to talk about losing the salvation that was offered in such love. Why would God remove something He offers unconditionally? It makes no sense at all.

Certainly there are those who will abuse God's mercy and forgiveness. But God's love is so pure that He will not go back on His word even to those who abuse their relationship with Him. He remains faithful to the faithless. Nothing can separate us from God's love. No one can snatch us from His hand. Where sin abounds, grace *super*abounds. Anything less would be less than unconditional.

Any time you begin to doubt God's love for you, immerse yourself again in the Scriptures that speak of God's love, His forgiveness, and His free offer of salvation and everlasting life. Ask the Lord to help you to believe even more fully that He loves you. As one person cried out to Jesus, "Lord, I believe; help my unbelief!" (Mark 9:24).

Do not let a doubt-induced fear paralyze you and keep you from experiencing full assurance of your salvation and God's love for you.

> • *Have you ever felt that God's love is too good to be true? Have you doubted God's love for you? Have you called out to God, saying, "Lord, help my unbelief"?*

_____

_____

Some begin to doubt God's love when they sin after they are born again and they experience God's chastening. They associate the pain and sorrow they feel with judgment and anger, rather than with love. The Lord chastens us out of His love, but what we *feel* when we are being chastened may not be feelings that *we* normally associate with love. A young child who is being spanked is likely *not* to think of his parent's love while the spanking is being administered, although the parent's love for the child never changes, and in fact, it is love that motivates the parent to discipline his child so that the child will experience a better future. What we *feel* is never a good gauge for what is *truth*. The truth remains that God loves us and His love toward us does not diminish, regardless of the severity of chastening we may receive.

What the Word Says	What the Word Says to Me
For the Lord will not cast off forever,	_____
Though He causes grief,	_____
Yet He will show compassion	_____
According to the multitude of His mercies.	_____
For He does not afflict willingly,	_____
Nor grieve the children of men (Lam. 3:31–33).	_____

I called on Your name, O LORD,
From the lowest pit.
You have heard my voice:
"Do not hide Your ear
From my sighing, from my cry for
help."
You drew near on the day I called
on You,
And said, "Do not fear!" (Lam.
3:55–57).

As many as I love, I rebuke and
chasten. Therefore be zealous and
repent (Rev. 3:19).

[The Lord said,] "Yes, I have
loved you with an everlasting love;
Therefore with lovingkindness I
have drawn you.
Again I will build you, and you
shall be rebuilt" (Jer. 31:3–4).

[Jesus said:] "Greater love has no
one than this, than to lay down
one's life for his friends. You are
My friends" (John 15:13–14).

Pride Can Rob Us of Assurance

The third great enemy of our assurance of salvation is our own
pride. It is an expression of pride to think or believe that *we* must
contribute something to our own salvation—that we can *do* something to augment the work of Jesus on the cross. So many Christians
try to compensate for their own sins. In the process, they eventually discover that they *cannot* do even those things that they want
to do and know they should do! A spirit of striving sets in, and soon
the person loses the joy of the Lord and becomes discouraged.

A person who is striving to do the "right things" in order to be
pleasing to God and to ensure his own salvation is a person who is
going to be far less fruitful in his life. He will not be fully yielded

to the Holy Spirit, so that the Holy Spirit might produce the fruit of His own character in his life. (See Gal. 5:22, 25.) A spirit of striving produces tension, anxiety, and frustration—none of which are attractive to the person who has not yet responded to the gospel of Jesus Christ.

The cure for pride, of course, is to bow before God in humility and say simply, "I surrender all. I give You all that I am, have, and ever will be or have. I am Yours. Do with me as You will." A person who truly surrenders all to the Lord will soon discover that he *receives* all of the Lord in return! When we seek to try to live life on our own, the Lord is free to endue us with His life.

Remaining Worthy?

Some Christians regard their good works as a means of remaining "worthy" of God's love and salvation. Friend, if that is your position today, I must tell you: You can *never* be worthy of God's ongoing salvation of your soul on the basis of your works. The fact is, nothing you ever did or thought to do made you "good" enough to deserve the death of Jesus Christ on the cross. Christ died for you while you were a sinner. If you had been capable of achieving perfection on your own, He would have had no reason to shed His blood for you. However, you are *not* capable of ever achieving perfection on your own or of transforming your own sin nature into a nature of righteousness before God. You were not worthy of your salvation, but praise God, Jesus Christ was worthy of winning that salvation for you! He took your place and He purchased for you a salvation that He then offered to you freely.

Now, as a believer in Christ Jesus, the Lord declares you worthy of eternal life. You are worthy of the Holy Spirit. You are now worthy because Jesus declares you to be worthy! Worthiness from God's perspective is *never* based upon what you have done, do, or will do. Worthiness is based solely on who Jesus is, what He has done, and what He declares on your behalf.

You can neither obtain nor ensure your salvation with good works; you can only receive God's salvation with a humble heart and submit your life to Him daily so that you might truly walk in His ways to the glory of His name.

- *In your life, have you fully surrendered all to Christ Jesus? Are you still trying to do the "right things" in order to gain God's approval? Are you still trying to be "worthy" of your salvation?*

_____

_____

What the Word Says

Seek those things which are above, where Christ is, sitting at the right hand of God. Set your mind on things above, not on things on the earth. For you died, and your life is hidden with Christ in God (Col. 3:1–3).

"God resists the proud,
But gives grace to the humble."
Therefore submit to God (James 4:6–7).

He who is mighty has done great things for me,
And holy is His name.
And His mercy is on those who fear Him
From generation to generation.
He has shown strength with His arm;
He has scattered the proud in the imagination of their hearts.
He has put down the mighty from their thrones,
And exalted the lowly.
He has filled the hungry with good things,

What the Word Says to Me

And the rich He has sent away
empty (Luke 1:49–53).

Choosing What You Will Believe

To a great extent, you have a choice to make. You can choose to receive forgiveness and live in freedom from guilt. You can choose to receive God's love and live in freedom from a doubt-induced fear. You can choose to humble yourself and trust God completely with your life. In making these choices, you can and *will* know with total *assurance* that your salvation is eternally secure.

On the other hand, you can choose to hold on to your guilt, nurse your doubts about God's love and remain paralyzed in fear, and continue to strive to "earn" your salvation. In making these choices, you will experience a great deal of frustration, discouragement, sorrow, and a lack of enthusiasm for the things of God. Furthermore, you will not have the "blessed assurance" that God desires for you. Your salvation may be eternally secure, but you will have none of the joy that comes in believing you are secure!

The Impact on Your Witness

The assurance that you have about your salvation directly impacts your witness for Jesus Christ. Those who *know* without a shadow of a doubt that they are eternally secure are those who have a great deal of boldness and freedom to share the gospel with others. Their lives attract sinners to Christ. Those who question their salvation and live without assurance are both reluctant and ineffective in their witness. What you believe about Christ's sacrifice for you will directly impact the degree to which you confess Christ to others.

Choose to place your trust squarely in God's love, the definitive sacrificial work of Jesus Christ on the cross, and in God's plan for your eternal life. The choice to trust is just that—a *choice* God calls you to make.

What the Word Says	What the Word Says to Me
"Here is the man who did not make God his strength, But trusted in the abundance of	------------------------------ ------------------------------ ------------------------------

his riches,
And strengthened himself in his
wickedness."
But I am like a green olive tree in
the house of God;
I trust in the mercy of God forever
and ever.
I will praise You forever,
Because You have done it;
And in the presence of Your saints
I will wait on Your name, for it is
good (Ps. 52:7–9).

Trust in the Lord with all your
heart,
And lean not on your own under-
standing;
In all your ways acknowledge
Him,
And He shall direct your paths.
Do not be wise in your own eyes;
Fear the Lord and depart from
evil.
It will be health to your flesh,
And strength to your bones (Prov.
3:5–8).

- *In what ways are you feeling challenged in your spirit regarding eternal security?*

CONCLUSION

ETERNALLY SECURE AND *FREE*!

I often meet people who say to me that they are content to "agree to disagree" on the issue of eternal security. I am not so agreeable! I know the bondage that a belief in falling from grace can create. For many years, I lived with the guilt and fear fostered by that view. Jesus said, "You shall know the truth, and the truth shall make you free" (John 8:32). Freedom comes from knowing the truth. Bondage results from missing it.

I know from experience that until you settle once and for all the question of whether or not you are eternally secure, joy and a deep peace in your soul will elude you. Fear and worry will hound you in the deepest recesses of your being. Therefore, my prayer is that God has used this study to convince you once and for all that if you have believed in Jesus Christ as providing the definitive, substitutionary, atoning sacrifice for your sin, and have received Jesus as your Savior, you *are* eternally secure in your relationship with God! You *have* everlasting life and a home in heaven. Nothing can strip your salvation from you.

God desires that you live in freedom, joy, and peace. Choose to desire what God desires. Accept Christ's death on the cross as payment in full. Your expression of faith in Jesus takes only a moment of time, but it seals you as a believer for all time!